CHILDCRAFT
THE HOW AND WHY LIBRARY

WHO
WE ARE

World Book, Inc.
a Scott Fetzer company
Chicago

World Book, Inc.
233 N. Michigan Avenue
Chicago, IL 60601

© 1996, 1995, 1994, 1993, 1991, 1990, 1989, 1987, 1986, 1985 World Book, Inc. © 1982, 1981, 1980, 1979, World Book-Childcraft International, Inc.
© 1976, 1974, 1973, 1971, 1970, 1969, 1968, 1965, 1964 Field Enterprises Educational Corporation.

International Copyright © 1996, 1995, 1994, 1993, 1991, 1990, 1989, 1987, 1986, 1985 World Book, Inc. International Copyright © 1982, 1981, 1980, 1979 World Book-Childcraft International, Inc. International Copyright © 1976, 1974, 1973, 1971, 1970, 1969, 1968, 1965, 1964 Field Enterprises Educational Corporation.

Childcraft—The How and Why Library ISBN 0-7166-0197-4
Who We Are ISBN 0-7166-0161-3
Library of Congress Catalog Card Number 98-75114
Printed in the United States of America
        2 3 4 5 6 7 8 9 06 05 04 03 02 01

Acknowledgments

Durkee, Sarah: "Thank Someone" by Sarah Durkee. *From Free To Be...A Family* © 1987 Ms. Foundation For Women. By permission.

Tolstoy, Alexi: "The Turnip" from *Russian Tales For Children* by Alexi Tolstoy. ©1947. Translated by Evgenia Schimanskaya. By permission of Routledge and Kegan Paul.

For information on other World Book products, visit our Web site at www.worldbook.com
For information on sales to schools and libraries in the United States, call 1-800-975-3250.
For information on sales to schools and libraries in Canada, call 1-800-837-5365.

Contents

Everyone is part of a group—a family, a neighborhood, a village, a town, our world. The people in your group are important to you in many ways.

Almost everyone in the world eats bread. But other food choices are very different—from reindeer milk to fried ants. Find out more about what we eat and how we eat it.

We all love to play. But we don't all play the same games. Sometimes our games are alike, and sometimes they are very different.

People learn in school. But how do people learn when they are not in a classroom?

People have certain ways of behaving that help them get along with one another. What are they?

Introduction

Who are you? When someone asks you that question, you may answer by saying your name. But there is much more to who you are than just your name. You are someone who spends time with other people, especially your family. You are also a member of your neighborhood, a citizen of your town. Some of what makes you who you are depends on where you live.

This book, *Who We Are,* explores where names come from and how people choose them. You may discover that the name your parents gave you has a special meaning. You will read about family activities and celebrations, including your special day—your birthday. You will see how the clothes you wear may give clues about who you are. You will find out more about neighborhoods, villages, and towns. You will take a closer look at what people eat, play, and learn.

There are many features in this book to help you find your way through it. You will find fun-filled facts in the boxes marked **Know It All!** You can amaze your friends with what you learn!

This book also has many activities that you can do at home. Look for the words **Try This!** over a colored ball. The activity that follows offers a way to learn more about who we are. For example, you can make some foods that may be new to you, such as bread called bruschetta from Italy or date bars from the Middle East. You can play the games Derrah and Mancala from Africa. Or you can learn to say "Hello" in many languages.

Each activity has a number from 1 to 3 in its colored ball. Activities with a 1 in a green ball are simplest to do. Those with a 2 inside a yellow ball may require a little adult help with tasks such as cutting or measuring. Activities with a 3 inside a red ball may need more adult help.

A Try This! activity that has a colorful border around its entire page is a little more complex or requires a few more materials. Take a moment to review the

Know It All! boxes have fun-filled facts.

Each activity has a number. The higher the number, the more adult help you may need.

An activity that has this colorful border is a little more complex than one without the border.

list of materials and to read through the instructions before you begin.

As you read this book, you will see that some words are printed in bold type, **like this.** These are words that might be new to you. You can find the meanings and pronunciations of these words in the **Glossary** at the back of the book. Turn to the **Index** to look up page numbers of subjects that interest you the most.

If you enjoy learning about who we are, find out more about it in other resources. Here are just a few of them. Check them out at a bookstore or at the library in your school or town.

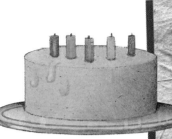

📖 **Children Just Like Me: Celebrations,** by Anabel Kindersley, 1997. *This big, beautiful book offers lively information on holidays and celebrations around the world.*

📖 **A Gift for Abuelita,** by Nancy Luenn, 1998. *Written in English and Spanish, this is a fictional story of a Mexican-American girl who prepares a gift for her deceased grandmother as her family celebrates the Day of the Dead.*

📖 **Festivals of the World: Netherlands,** by Joyce van Fenema, 1998. *This book discusses the festivals and culture of the Netherlands. Check out the other books in the "Festivals of the World" series.*

📖 **Grandfather's Journey,** by Allen Say, 1993. *This beautifully illustrated book is filled with touching memories of the author's grandfather's life in America and Japan.*

📖 **How to Make an Apple Pie and See the World,** by Marjorie Priceman, 1994. *A little girl finds herself taking a fanciful trip around the world to pick up ingredients to make a pie.*

📖 **The Kids' Multicultural Cookbook: Food & Fun Around the World,** by Deanna F. Cook, 1995. *This is a big, user-friendly kids' book filled with fun, easy-to-do recipes from other countries.*

📖 **A Ride on Mother's Back,** by Emery Bernard, 1996. *You will take a journey around the world and learn how mothers and fathers from different cultures care for their babies.*

📖 **To Be a Kid,** by Maya Ajmera and John D. Ivanko, 1997. *In this photographic essay of children around the world, you will see that being a kid means just about the same thing no matter where you live.*

📖 **A True Book of Ellis Island,** by Patricia Ryon Quiri, 1998. *For more than 50 years, Ellis Island served as an immigrant station for those wishing to make a new life in the United States.*

📖 **Two Lands, One Heart: An American Boy's Journey to his Mother's Vietnam,** by Jeremy Schmidt and Ted Wood, 1995. *A boy accompanies his mother on her trip back to the homeland she fled in wartime.*

📖 **Work,** by Ann Morris, 1998. *This collection of photos of people at their work takes you on a trip around the world.*

Families and Neighbors

Every child comes into the world with special gifts to share. Your good ideas, sense of humor, kind heart, and smile are needed by people everywhere. Your family, friends, and neighbors help you learn to share these things.

These people help you learn about life. With them, you discover the world that is waiting for you.

You have many other important people in your life too. Farmers grow healthful food to feed you, doctors and nurses help keep your body strong, and police officers watch over you. Artists, authors, and inventors bring wonderful ideas to life for you to enjoy.

All around the world, every day, children are growing, playing, and learning. And wherever there are children, people help them grow.

What Is a Family?

This Thai family plays a game together.

Look around you. Who are the people who care for you? They are your family. Families are people who love and help each other, whether they live together or in different places.

Families can include mothers, fathers, children, grandparents, brothers, sisters, aunts, uncles, cousins, and friends. A family can be any size—just two people, or twenty, or more.

Some children live with two parents, some live with one parent. Some children live with grandparents or with a foster family. Other children live with a parent and a stepparent and other children.

A European family enjoys a picnic.

Do you have brothers or sisters? Do you live with your aunt or your cousins? There are all kinds of families, and no two are exactly alike.

Inuit (IN oo iht) families in northern Canada spend all their time together. In the summer, families hunt and fish together.

An American family shares responsibility for their pet together.

On a **kibbutz** in Israel, all the parents may live together in one house while all the children live together in another. The children go to school and play together, while parents work on the community farm.

These children on an Israeli kibbutz go to school.

An Ashanti (uh SHAN tee) boy in Ghana (GAH nuh), Africa, lives with many mothers. He lives in a house with his mother, his grandmother, and his mother's sisters and their children. All the children are like brothers and sisters. The boy's father comes to visit, but he lives in his own mother's house.

An Ashanti boy in Ghana lives in a house with his mother and her family.

In Japan, grandparents often live with their oldest son and his family. The grandmother helps care for the children. In Norway, many farms have two houses. One house is for the grandparents, and one is for their son or daughter and their grandchildren.

A Mongolian family lives in a house called a yurt, a type of tent made out of felt.

On the island of Borneo (BOHR nee oh), all the people in a Dayak (DAY ak) village live together in one long house. Each family is also part of the village family.

Families come in all sizes and styles. Wherever they live, families are people who care for and help one another.

TRY THIS! **1**

Make a list of your family members. Now add the names of friends and neighbors who feel like family to you.

These children in Borneo live together in one long house.

Where Do Names Come From?

Your first name is the name people call you. Your family chose it for you when you were born. Your last name is called your family name. Where did that name come from?

The earliest people had only first names. Their family and friends knew them by those first names.

About 800 years ago, kings and other royal people in Europe began to use last names to show that they were special. Soon, everyone in Europe took a last name.

How did people choose a family name? Sometimes peoples' names described where they lived. *Castle, Castillo, Castello,*

Long ago, many family names described where people lived. So, the Hillman family were people who lived on a hill. We still use these old names today.

HILLMAN

SILVA

LAKE

FIELD

BROOKS

BURRIS

STREETER

The name *Russell* means "red-haired."

Zamecki, Burke, Borg, and *Burris* are names in several languages that meant a person lived near a castle. Names like *Wood, Woods, Atwood, Smallwood, Boyce, DuBois, Holt, Shaw,* and *Silva* meant a person lived near a forest.

Can you guess what the names *Streeter, Lane, Strass,* and *Estrada* meant? They meant someone who lived by a road.

Sometimes people's names described what they looked like. If people had light-colored hair, they might be named *White, Wise, Weiss, Whitehead, Whitlock, Whitman, Blanchard,* or *Bannon.* And if they had red hair, their name might be *Reed, Reid, Roth, Russell,* or *Flynn.*

Bliss, Blythe, Froh, Merriman, Blaha, or *Allegretti* are names that mean "happy."

Some people were named after personal characteristics. Someone as smart as a fox might be called Ms. Fox.

A person who's as smart as a fox might be called *Fox, Fuchs, Todd,* or *Volpe.* A brave person might be called *Lion, Lyon, Lyons, Loewe,* or *Leon.*

Some names described what people did or where they were from. A baker might take the name *Baker, Baxter, Fournier, Piekarz,* or *Boulanger.* A blacksmith who makes horseshoes might be called *Smith, Schmidt, Lefevre, Ferraro, Kowalski, Kovacs,* or *MacGowan.*

Robert's child might take the name *Roberts.* John's son becomes *Johnson,* Nels' son is *Nelson.* Davey's, Harry's, and Will's children take the names *Davis, Harris,* and *Wilson.*

Some "son" names end in *-sohn, -wicz, -vich,* or *-ak. Mac-, Mc-,* or *Fitz-* means "the son of."

Some family names described people's jobs. The name *Baxter* comes from a word that means "baker."

Some children were known by their father's name. So, people called the son of Wil, *Wil's son*. Later, this name became *Wilson*.

A new person in town might be *Newman, Newcomb, Doyle, Doran,* or *Dowell.* They all mean "new man."

TRY THIS!

1

Ask a family member about your family's name. What does it mean? What language is it from? Was it ever spelled differently?

Doyle

A person new to town might take the name *Doyle,* which means "new man."

17

Who Are You?

Are you Alex? Sophie? David? Maria? Naomi? Abi?

The English name *John* is *Ivan* in Russian, *Juan* in Spanish, *Iahaja* in Turkish, *Johann* in German, and *Sean* in Irish.

The name *Mary* is *Marie, Moira, Miriam,* and *Maria* in different languages.

Alfreda means "wise adviser."

You've worn your name since you were born. How does it fit you? Almost every name has a meaning behind it. What about yours?

The name *Alfreda* means "wise adviser." *Helen* means "light."

Wendy means "wanderer."

Louis means "great warrior"

TRY THIS!
1

How did you get your name? Who chose it? Were you named for someone special? Ask a grown-up. You may find some interesting answers!

The name *Thang* means
"triumph." *Thuy* is "gracious."

Abdu is "Servant of Allah."
Allah is the Muslim name
for "God." *Kossi* means
"boy born on Sunday."

Henry is "master of a house."
Richard means "harsh king."
Eric means "royal."

Hannah means "grace." *Wendy*
is a "wanderer." *George* is a
"farmer." *Louis* is a "great warrior."
Barbara means "stranger." *Ellen*
means "bright."

Look up your name in a book of baby
names. You'll find one at the library.
Check out the names of your family
and friends. Some meanings may fit,
some may seem funny!

Abdu means
"Servant of Allah."

George means "farmer."

Eric means "royal."

19

Many children help cook for their family. This boy in the United States is helping to make strawberry jam.

Children in many families care for their younger brothers and sisters. This girl in Turkey is keeping an eye on her little brother.

What Families Do Together

Families work, learn, grow, and have fun together—each in its own way. Everywhere in the world, family members love and help one another.

Many families **worship** together. These children are taking part in a Shinto (SHIHN toh) religious **ceremony** in Japan.

Families play and explore together in all kinds of ways. Some may visit faraway places. This family is hiking in the mountains in France.

Many families work together. They grow crops and take care of their homes. These children of Fiji in the South Pacific are helping at harvest time.

In families, people teach and learn from each other. This boy on Africa's Ivory Coast is getting a drum lesson.

Students wear a special cap and gown during the graduation ceremony at many North American schools.

How Do You Celebrate?

Start your own tradition. Send a card, make a special treat, volunteer to help someone, or sing a song. You could mark the first flower of spring, a good report card, a full moon, or your pet's birthday!

TRY THIS!

1

People use **traditions** to mark important days. On special days for your family, there will be certain ceremonies, special foods, and maybe even presents. These are your traditions.

Family traditions mark big life changes and smaller ones, too. Some families have traditions for the first or last day of each school year, including eating special meals or wearing special outfits. School graduations are big days for many families. People **celebrate** them with photographs and parties.

Traditions welcome new babies to the world. Some **Christian** families take their babies to church to be baptized. The ceremony marks their entry into the Christian faith. In Japan's Shinto religion, a mother takes her baby to a shrine to "show" it to the gods and give thanks for its life.

In Swaziland (SWAH zee land), Africa, parents burn animal hair and animal skins. Then they hold a new baby in the smoke to give it lifelong protection from wild animals. Among the Lao of Southeast Asia, it is a tradition to rub a baby's body with salt to protect it from evil.

Weddings are also filled with traditions. An Arab bride arrives at her wedding hidden in a tent on top of a camel. The groom pretends to run away, and his friends catch him. Then the wedding ceremony begins.

In Japan, some mothers take their babies to Shinto shrines to give thanks for them.

A well-hidden bride rides to her wedding on a camel in Tunisia in North Africa.

This bride is wearing traditional clothing called a kimono at a Shinto wedding in Japan.

At a Shinto wedding in Japan, the bride wears a kimono (kuh MOHN uh) and covers her face with white powder. The bride and groom must take nine sips of rice wine together.

This couple in the United States lights a candle together at their wedding as a symbol of their unity.

In an American tradition, some brides wear "something old, something new, something borrowed, something blue." In North America, brides traditionally wear a long white dress and veil. In India, brides wear red and cover themselves with gold jewelry.

Traditions also help us say good-bye and show respect when someone

When a Hindu dies on the island of Bali, the body is burned on a platform decorated with flowers. A statue of a cow, a sacred animal for Hindus, may be included.

dies. In North America and Europe, a dead person's body may be placed in a coffin and buried. Sometimes the body is burned rather than buried. The person's ashes may be placed in a vase, or urn.

In the **Hindu** (HIN doo) religion, tradition calls for a body to be burned. In India, the ashes are thrown into the holy Ganges (GAN jeez) River.

At a funeral in the United States, people often wear black to show respect and sadness. In China, people wear white for mourning.

When Is Your Special Day?

Throughout the world, people have different traditions for marking the passing of years.

In the United States, one tradition is to blow out candles on a birthday cake and make a wish.

In China, everyone adds a year to their age at the same time— on the Chinese New Year, which is between the end of January and the end of February.

In the Philippines, birthdays are celebrated when a child is 1, 7, 14, and 21 years old.

In some Native American tribes, a special ceremony is held when children are given their tribal name at around age 4.

Many people have traditions to mark the end of childhood. A Tamil (TAM uhl) girl of Sri Lanka gets to wear a sari, the beautiful dress of a woman, when she is about 13.

Women wave candles in a dish of food before a Tamil girl during a ceremony that marks the end of her childhood.

When a Jewish boy is 13, he has his *bar mitzvah* (bahr MIHTS vuh). A Jewish girl has her *bat mitzvah* (baht MIHTS vuh) at age 12. Both boys and girls read from holy books and answer religious questions.

In Brazil, Mexico, and other Hispanic countries, a girl's 15th birthday is very special. The family holds a big **coming-of-age** party. This is called a quinceañera (KEEN say ahn YAIR ah).

A boy reads from a holy book on his bar mitzvah.

KNOW It All!

The idea of putting candles on birthday cakes goes back to **ancient** Greece. The Greeks worshiped many gods and goddesses. Among them was one called Artemis (AHR tuh mihs). Artemis was the goddess of the moon. The Greeks celebrated her birthday once each month by bringing special cakes to her temple. The cakes were round, like a full moon. And, because the moon glows with light, the cakes were decorated with lighted candles.

Do Clothes Talk?

Women from Kenya, Africa, wear clothing with bright colors and bold patterns.

What do your clothes say about you? They're not talking? Are you sure? Clothes tell a lot about who you are and where you live.

Many people wear **folk costumes** for religious festivals and ceremonies. Different **cultures** have different folk costumes.

These Native American girls keep their culture alive by wearing traditional Indian clothing and jewelry.

On holidays in Scotland, men dress in kilts—knee-length, pleated wool skirts. Each kilt is woven in a special plaid called a tartan. Each Scottish clan, or group of families, has its own tartan.

Women in Guatemala weave all the colors of the rainbow into their traditional clothing.

The silver ornaments and jewelry of these people on the island of Borneo in Malaysia show that they are important in their village. They are dressed for a special celebration.

On special days, Japanese people wear silk kimonos with beautiful **embroidery**.

Colorful embroidery decorates these traditional Romanian costumes.

These women in India decorate their clothes with tiny mirrors.

American teenagers spend a lot of time together. They usually wear clothes that are very much like the ones that their group of friends wears.

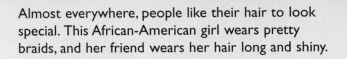

Almost everywhere, people like their hair to look special. This African-American girl wears pretty braids, and her friend wears her hair long and shiny.

Look Your Best

People everywhere dress to protect themselves from the weather. They also dress to look good.

Clothes aren't needed in the steamy forests of Brazil. But jewelry is very important. Forest **dwellers** in Brazil make beautiful jewelry out of treasures

In New Guinea, some people wear necklaces made of seashells.

Egyptians long, long ago placed gold jewelry and precious gems in the tombs of their kings, who were called pharaohs. This was to help the pharaoh have good fortune in the afterlife.

found in the jungle—stones, bones, teeth, claws, and feathers. For colorful ear ornaments, they may use the bright feathers of the toucan.

In Kenya, Africa, the Masai (mah SY) people wear necklaces and headdresses made from hundreds of brightly colored beads. They thread the beads together in patterns.

People have worn jewelry since long ago times. Sometimes they thought jewelry could bring good luck. Sometimes it was worn to show how important a person was or as part of a religious ceremony.

Jewelry is most often used as a decoration. When you wear a new watch or tie beads in your hair, your jewelry shows the world who you are and how you feel.

An Indian girl may dress up with beads, sequins, and flowers.

Neighborhoods, Villages, and Towns

A neighborhood is a place where people live together. Every neighborhood is special to the people who live there.

Do you live in the middle of a busy city or in a tiny farm town? Are you in a suburb in America or do you live in the African desert? No matter where you live, you have neighbors. They might be very close by, or they may be miles away.

Do you know your neighbors? How are they like you? What do you do together? How do you help one another?

Some people live in the desert in Africa. They live in tents that are easy to take down and move. A whole group will move together, neighbors and all.

Many people in Australia live on ranches raising cattle and sheep. Ranches in Australia can be many miles apart, so people don't see their neighbors often.

In towns and small cities families live near each other. Neighbors are always nearby.

People who live in big cities live close to their neighbors and see people all the time.

What Happens Where You Live?

Neighbors keep things lively in every kind of neighborhood. What do your neighbors do?

These Indian women from Guatemala in Central America weave beautiful rugs and carpets.

These girls pick tea leaves in northeast India.

Many people in Newfoundland live near the ocean and fish for a living.

Some boys from Tanzania in eastern Africa help their families farm cattle on the grasslands.

The Amish are religious people in the United States who live together in farm communities. When an Amish farmer needs a new barn, all the Amish neighbors come together to build it.

Shoppers fill the street at the Petticoat Lane market in London, England.

Thank Someone

Who are the people in your family and neighborhood? How do you thank them for helping out or being a friend? This poem by Sarah Durkee has some ideas.

Mom put down the paper
just to help me find my shoe.
Kim likes chocolate doughnuts,
so her cousin gave her two.
Grampa played with Julio,
took him to the park.
If you forgot to thank someone,
say thank you in the dark.

Thank the moon,
thank the sun,
most of all
Thank someone.
Thank the stars
high above,
one for
everyone you love.

Gretchen taught a funny song
to Jack and Eleanor.
Ed brought Andy comics
when he had to stay indoors.
Mrs. Rose helped Dana
when she waded out too deep.
If you forgot to thank someone,
say thank you in your sleep.

Thank the moon,
thank the sun,
most of all
Thank someone.
Thank the stars
high above,
one for
everyone you love.

Friends are like a family,
and families are like friends.
All the world's your family;
the chain will never end.
When the night is lonely
and we're feelin' miles apart,
if you forgot to thank someone
say thank you in your heart.

Thank the moon,
thank the sun,
most of all
Thank someone.
Thank the stars
high above,
one for
everyone you love.

What Do We Eat?

Are you hungry? Would you like some alligator eggs? How about strawberry ice cream? Raw meat in red-pepper sauce? Maybe a few fried ants?

Do those sound yummy or yucky? It all depends on who you are and where in the world you live.

Everyone, everywhere, must eat to live. But *what* people eat, *how* they cook their food, and even *when* they eat can be very different.

Bread, the World Favorite

These women on the island of Cyprus share an oven to bake their bread.

Do you eat bread? Most people in the world do. In fact, bread is the world's number-one food choice.

Bread is sometimes called "the staff of life" because it is such an important food.

46

Bread is made from **grain,** such as wheat, corn, oats, barley, rye, or rice. First, the grain is ground into flour. The flour is mixed with other ingredients, which may include water, salt, and **yeast,** to make a dough. Then it is baked.

Bread comes in all shapes and textures. It can rise and be fluffy, like yeast breads or quick breads, or it can lie flat as a pancake. It can be shaped in a loaf, twisted into doughnuts, rolled into rolls, or cut into crackers.

Soft or crusty bread is preferred in the United States, Canada, and Europe, but flat bread is common elsewhere. In Mexico, people eat flat cornmeal or wheat tortillas (tor TEE yuhz). In China, thin rice bread is wrapped around other foods. In India, the flat chapatti (chuh PAT ee) is baked from ground wheat. In Turkey, a pancake-shaped *pita* (PEE tuh) makes a tasty pocket for meat and vegetables. Crusty, long, thin baguette (buh GEHT) loaves are popular in France. Dark, chewy rye bread is a favorite in Russia and Germany.

Wheat is the most popular bread grain because it grows well in many places.

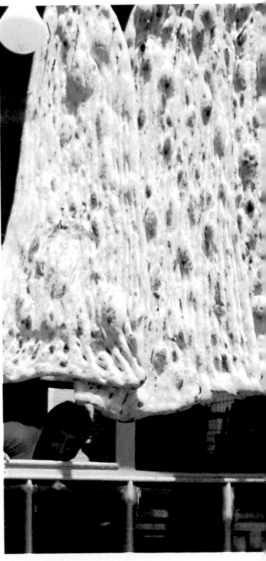

Bread baked in thin, flat sheets hangs outside a bakery in Iran.

Rice Is Nice

Rice grows best in fields covered with water, such as this one in Thailand.

Growing rice is hard but important work. In many Asian countries, the word for *rice* is also the word for *food*.

An old Chinese story tells how rice became good to eat. At one time, the grains of the rice plant were empty and not good as food. One day a goddess saw people suffering because they were always hungry. To help the people, the goddess secretly filled the grains with milk. That made the rice good to eat. From then on, people were not so hungry.

KNOW It All!

Rice is much, much more than food. Rice is used to make alcohol, paper, cosmetics, glue, starch, paste, and vinegar. Rice stalks are used to make brooms, hats, mats, rope, sacks, and sandals.

Harvesttime means
lots of hard work in
the fields for these rice
farmers in China.

The story shows how important rice is. For more than half the people in the world, rice has been the main course at every meal for hundreds of years.

Southeast Asia's hot, wet climate is perfect for growing rice. Farm families in China, Vietnam, and other rice-growing countries plant young rice seedlings in large, flooded fields. When the rice begins to ripen, they drain the water from the fields. At harvesttime, they gather and dry the rice.

Reindeer Milk and Yak Butter

Yaks are large and strong. They are used for many things, including milk and butter.

"**W**here I live, milk comes from the reindeer," said Paavo. "My father has the finest herd of reindeer in Lapland. We eat reindeer meat, and we use reindeer skin to make tents and clothes. And the reindeer's milk makes the best butter and cheese!"

Vashni comes from India. "In my village, milk comes from the water buffalo," she said. "Everybody drinks buffalo milk."

"I live on a cattle station in Australia," said George, "and we don't milk reindeer or buffalo there. Our milk comes from cows."

Abdu then told the others about his country. "In Saudi Arabia, all the children of my tribe drink camel milk. Camels have very bad tempers, but very good milk."

"If you want good cheese, try some Greek feta," said Orestes. "My mother makes it from goats' milk."

Jamal just smiled. "In Tibet where I live, we get our milk from the yak. I can't believe any other milk could taste as good. And as for yak butter—it's wonderful."

This girl from Lapland in northern Europe is milking a reindeer. She will use the milk to make cheese.

At the cheese market at Alkmaar in the Netherlands, you can try all kinds of cheeses made from cows' milk.

radish

lettuce

beet

Eat Your Vegetables

Brightly colored plants add crunch to your lunch—and healthy vitamins, too. No wonder parents everywhere say, "Eat your vegetables!"

What veggies do you munch? That partly depends on where you live and

In Papua New Guinea, people enjoy fresh picked corn.

A healthy meal includes vegetables.

Olives grow well in sunny countries like Greece, Spain, and Italy. Italians eat green, black, stuffed, or **pickled** olives. They make oil from olives, too.

what plants grow there. In Indonesia, many people enjoy *asinan,* a tasty dish usually made of mustard leaves, bean sprouts, bean paste, radishes, and peanuts. All these plants **thrive** in the hot, wet climate. In China, the root of the lotus flower is sliced for salads.

People serve lots of cabbage, carrots, and potatoes in Britain, where the weather is wet and mild. In sunny Mexico, people eat red peppers, green peppers, and corn.

Beets grow well in cool places, and cooks in Poland, Russia, and Scandinavia make a delicious beet soup called borscht (borsht).

Vegetables make a colorful display at a market in Mexico.

This woman is cooking an African favorite—squash.

Right now, wonderful vegetables from far away are waiting at your store. Try a new veggie today! With so many colorful, crunchy choices, you might want to eat *only* vegetables!

Food from the Sea

In Alaska, some people dry fish as a way to preserve it.

Good news for good eaters! An ocean covers more than 70 percent of our planet, and it is filled with plant and animal life. It has something for everyone. Enjoy fish of all kinds—sardines, mackerel, salmon, and herring—and other seafood, such as oysters, clams, crabs, lobsters, shrimp, and octopus. How about a shark steak?

How do you like your seafood? In Sweden, you can try pickled herring,

Raw fish with vegetables is a favorite Japanese meal.

smoked salmon, or baked halibut. In Japan, look for thin, cold slices of something pink on your plate. It's tasty *sashimi* (sah SHEE mee)—raw fish. You also can fill your plate with vitamin-rich sea vegetables. Seaweed is a popular dish in Japan.

For thousands of years, people everywhere have set out to sea in small boats to catch their supper. Today, huge modern fishing fleets have electronic equipment for finding fish.

People catch lobsters in cagelike traps. Shrimp, crabs, and some fish are caught in nets. Oysters are scooped up by machines called dredgers.

When a lobster crawls into a trap, it's caught!

A Turkish fisherman sells his catch from his boat in the city of Istanbul.

A Spanish butcher shop displays different meats.

Is Meat on the Menu?

Cattle are raised in South America for the meat we call beef.

Are you a meat-eater? If you are, what kind of meat do you like? Beef? Pork? Chicken? Lamb? Where you live might determine what kind of meat you like—and how much meat you eat.

The United States and Argentina raise lots of cattle, and people eat lots of beef. China raises the most pigs, and pork is popular there. In New Zealand, sheep and lambs are plentiful, including on the dinner table.

The Masai people of eastern Africa live by raising cattle. They get almost all their food from cows. However, they seldom eat meat. They live mostly on the milk and blood of cows.

Your religious beliefs may decide whether you eat meat. In Pakistan, most of the people are Muslims, and they don't eat pork. Orthodox Jews all around the world choose not to eat pork or **shellfish**. The Jains (jynz), a religious group in India, eat no meat at all.

Everywhere in the world, some people make a personal choice not to eat meat. People who do not eat meat are called vegetarians (vehj uh TAIR ee uhnz).

Australians raise sheep for their wool and for lamb meat.

In Pakistan, most people don't eat pork, but they enjoy lamb. Lamb kebabs are pieces of lamb cooked on a stick with slices of tomato, green pepper, and onion.

In Vermont, "sugaring off" means pouring maple sugar on snow and eating it.

What's for Dessert?

Do you have a "sweet tooth"? You do if you like candy, puddings, and other sugary treats. People everywhere find ways to satisfy a "sweet tooth."

Children in China like "drawn-wire apple." The apple is cooked in sweet, sticky toffee. When a piece of apple is lifted from the hot dish, the toffee cools and stretches in thin strips like wire.

In Spain, children eat colorful dragons made of marzipan, a type of candy made of almond paste and sugar.

Some "main course" foods can be turned into treats. Sweet potatoes are made into candy in Mexico and *camote-cues,* a sweet snack for children, in the Philippines.

In Myanmar, children love a chewy treat called *khaw pyin*, made of rice and sesame seeds. Also in Southeast Asia, many treats are made with coconut.

In North America, maple-tree sap is boiled to make syrup. And everywhere, bees are busy making honey all the time. People add these sweets to breads, cakes, and other foods.

Take good care of your sweet tooth— and all your other teeth too!

Mexican children delight in their fancy sweet potato candy.

This tasty coconut treat is served in a palm leaf in Indonesia.

On a seashore in Sicily, Italy, boys gather for a meal of boiled octopus.

What's Cooking?

It's dinnertime, and delicious smells are drifting through the air.

Some foods you can simply pick and eat, like a peach. Other foods need to be cooked for hours over a hot fire. People in different **cultures** have discovered many tasty ways to prepare their food. Dinner might be served raw, fried, boiled, or grilled indoors or outdoors.

Tonight, you're having fish and vegetables. How do you like them? Raw, boiled, fried, baked, grilled, stir-fried, roasted, or stewed?

In China, Wang Kow watches as his mother pours peanut oil into a deep, round frying pan called a wok. When the oil is hot, she adds meat and vegetables and tosses them as they cook. She is stir-frying the food.

Alex helps his father turn the steaks and sausages on their backyard grill in Sydney, Australia. They're having a cookout.

We often cook food to make it taste better. Cooking meat also makes it safer to eat. Vegetables are cooked to make them softer. Dough is baked to make cakes, cookies, and bread. Soups are **simmered** to blend the flavors of their ingredients together.

A woman dishes a serving of hot, spicy soup at a floating market in Bangkok, Thailand.

An Inuit woman scrapes maggots from the inside of a caribou skin for a meal.

Seaweed, Snails, and Frozen Fish Eyes

Suppose you were offered seaweed, snails, or frozen fish eyes. Would you turn up your nose in **disgust?** Or would you say, "Yes, please!"?

Food usually comes from plants or animals, and there are many kinds of plants and animals in this world. Some types of plants and animals do well in cold cities. Other types grow only in rain forests. What people eat often depends on the plants and animals that are near them.

Japanese women harvest seaweed to be dried and eaten.

Spine-covered sea urchins are considered a tasty treat in France, where people eat the insides raw with bread.

In Japan, seaweed is an important vegetable. It is part of many meals. In Wales, seaweed is cooked with oatmeal and eaten with bacon. Maybe you eat seaweed. Some jellylike stuff that comes from seaweed is used in many ice creams and jellies.

Snails baked in garlic and butter is a famous meal from France. It's called *escargot*. Sea urchins—raw—are also popular there. Many **Inuit** like to eat frozen fish eyes.

Do you want ants? Honeypot ants drink a sugary liquid from plants called honeydew. They drink so much of it that they look like little walking honeypots. In Australia and Mexico, people pop the sweet bugs into their mouths or spread them on toast.

A honeypot ant filled with sweet honeydew is an Australian treat.

Would you like to eat a frog?

Australian **aborigines** (ab uh RIHJ uh neez) like witchetty grubs, the larvae of beetles and moths.

Bird's-nest soup is a special Chinese dish. It is made from the nests of birds called swifts. To hold the nests together, the birds use their saliva. This makes the soup chewy!

In West Africa, where people eat few cooked desserts, a favorite treat is sugar cane! Children simply chew a piece of the plant, which grows in West African forests.

Certain foods may seem strange to you simply because you have not learned to eat them. But people around the world eat—and like—many different kinds of foods.

This tasty dish is a plate of cooked frog legs. It's a favorite in France.

Fingers, Forks, and Sticks

Some meals, like a hamburger and French fries in the United States, *above*, are best eaten with the fingers. Other meals, like this soup being served to a German family, *left*, are best eaten with a spoon.

When guests come for dinner, should you stick your hand in the serving bowl, or use a knife and fork at your own plate? At mealtime, should you sit on the floor, or sit on your chair at the table?

Well, your table manners will depend on where you are. People in different cultures have different eating **customs.**

If you are American or European, you probably eat from your own plate and use a knife, fork, and spoon. But you probably eat some foods, such as sandwiches, with your fingers.

Many Arab families eat from one serving bowl. They eat with only the right hand, whether they use fingers or spoons. In Ethiopia, people use pieces of bread to scoop up food from a common bowl.

In Japan and China, most people pick up their food with chopsticks. The food is served in small pieces, so knives aren't needed.

Americans and Europeans sit on chairs at a table when they eat. In the Middle East, Africa, and Asia, people often sit on the floor or outside, on the ground.

The members of this Arab family sit in a circle to spoon their food from the same bowl.

You can learn to use chopsticks at home. Get a pair of chopsticks and a dish of bite-sized food, such as pineapple chunks or bits of broccoli.

TRY THIS! 1

1. To hold your chopsticks, tuck the first chopstick under your thumb. Rest it firmly on your fourth finger. (Some people use their middle fingers instead.)

1.

2. Place the second chopstick between your index finger and thumb. Hold it like a pencil and move it up and down while the first chopstick stays still.

2.

3. Pick up food with your chopsticks just as a bird picks up food with its beak.

3.

What Are Silly Foods?

Does your family enjoy eating toad in the hole, heaven and earth, or hush puppies? Millions of people do!

Every country has some foods with funny-sounding names. Check out these examples, then think of some fun food names you know.

Toad in the hole (United Kingdom) is a sausage baked in a batter of flour, milk, and eggs. When cooked, the sausage looks like a toad peeking out of a hole.

Hush puppies (United States) are small balls of cornmeal fried in deep fat. A favorite snack in the South, they were sometimes fed to puppies to keep them quiet.

toad in the hole

hush puppy

Heaven and earth (Germany) is a side dish that combines apples, which grow on trees (heaven), with potatoes, which grow in the ground (earth).

Egg snowballs (Brazil) is a dessert made of beaten egg whites cooked into balls and placed on a pool of lemony sauce.

Bubble and squeak (United Kingdom) is a mixture of meat and cabbage or other greens that gets its name from the noises it makes in the frying pan.

Dragon's whiskers (China) are made from oolong tea packed in tiny, strawlike bundles and tied with red ribbon. *Oolong* is from the Chinese word for "black dragon." The tied-up package looks like a Chinese dragon with whiskers.

dragon whiskers

Try It, You'll Like It!

All this talk about food is enough to make you hungry—and curious. Well, start sampling! Here are some favorite recipes from other countries.

Be sure to ask a grown-up to assist you in cooking—and eating—your multicultural meal!

Note to adults: Most of these recipes require adult supervision in assembling ingredients and using the oven. However, all the recipes center on fun tasks that can easily be accomplished by children, including stirring, rolling balls, and flattening things.

Limonada (Lemonade)

Lemons and limes are natural fruity thirst quenchers. Lemon and lime drinks are popular in many places around the world. Makes 10 servings.

You Will Need:

- 1 1/2 cups (360 milliliters) lemon or lime juice (seeds removed)

- 1/2 cup (120 milliliters) corn syrup or to taste (ready-made or frozen lemonade can be substituted for first two ingredients)

- 2 small spoonfuls canned apricot nectar water from the world food section of your grocery store

- 8 12-oz. (360-milliliter) bottles of clear carbonated water

- crushed ice to fill 10 glasses

- 10 peppermint sprigs

- a pitcher or large bowl

- a long-handled spoon

- 10 glasses

- clean hands

What To Do:

1. Put the lemon or lime juice in a pitcher. Add the syrup and apricot nectar water, then mix well.

2. Fill each glass with crushed ice. Add about 1/4 cup (60 milliliters) of the juice mixture to each glass and fill to the top with carbonated water.

3. Garnish each drink with a mint sprig.

You Will Need:

1 loaf of Italian bread sliced lengthwise

2 or 3 chopped tomatoes

3-4 spoonfuls of olive oil

salt

about 12 chopped up basil leaves

serving plate

medium mixing bowl

bread knife

serving spoon

clean hands

Bruschetta (broo SKEH tuh)

Italian people like to eat their meals one course at a time, starting with an appetizer and working their way to the pasta or main dish. They may start their meal with an appetizer like this bruschetta. Makes six servings.

What To Do:

1. Ask an adult to help toast the bread. Lay the two sides open in the broiler for a few minutes until crispy. Then put them on a plate.

2. Put the tomatoes in the bowl.

3. Add the olive oil, a couple dashes of salt, and the basil to the tomatoes. Mix well.

4. Spoon the tomato mixture evenly over the toasted bread. Let it sit for 5 or 10 minutes so the flavors can soak into the bread.

5. Cut the bread into sections and serve.

Fufu (Sweet Potato Balls)

TRY THIS! 2

Sweet potatoes and yams are vegetables that grow underground. They are important foods in many countries. In Ghana, fufu is a national dish made with yams. Makes 12 to 18 balls.

What To Do:

1. Put the sweet potatoes or yams in the saucepan with the water. Ask an adult to bring the water to a boil. Then cover the pan and let the water simmer for about 40 minutes or until the potatoes are tender.

2. Remove the potatoes or yams from the heat and allow them to cool. Peel the potatoes, and then cut them into chunks. Using a potato masher or electric blender, mash the potatoes into a smooth paste. Mix with nutmeg, red pepper, salt, and pepper.

3. Wash your hands, then moisten them with water.

4. Roll the mixture in the **palms** of your hands. Shape the mixture into balls the size of golf balls.

You Will Need:

4 or 5 skin-on sweet potatoes or yams

6 cups (1.5 liters) water

1 teaspoon ground nutmeg

1 teaspoon ground red cayenne pepper, more or less to taste

onions, garlic, or peanuts (optional)

a medium saucepan with lid

a large mixing bowl

a potato masher or electric blender

a mixing spoon

clean hands

5. Place the balls side by side on a serving platter. Keep them at room temperature until they are ready to serve. Some people sprinkle their fufu with chopped onions, garlic, or peanuts.

Date Bars

A date is an oval-shaped fruit covered by tough skin. It may be yellow, orange, red, or green. Its thick, sweet flesh surrounds a single large seed. Dates are a popular treat throughout the Middle East. Makes 16 bars.

What To Do:

1. Preheat the oven to 350 °F.

2. Put the oats, flour, baking powder, salt, and cinnamon in a bowl and mix well. In another bowl, put the brown sugar, butter, and eggs.

You Will Need:

1 cup rolled oats, plain or instant

1/2 cup all-purpose flour

1/2 teaspoon baking powder

1/2 teaspoon salt

1 teaspoon cinnamon

1/2 cup dark brown sugar

1 cup melted butter or margarine

2 eggs, beaten

1 cup finely chopped pitted dates (cut with scissors)

1 cup chopped walnuts, peanuts, or pecans (optional)

1/2 cup confectioners' sugar for garnish

a large mixing bowl

a mixing spoon

a greased 8-inch square baking pan

clean hands

3. Add the wet ingredients to the dry ingredients. Mix well. Add the dates and nuts.

4. Spread the batter into the baking pan and bake in the oven for about 35 minutes, until firm.

5. Remove the pan from the oven. While it is still warm, sprinkle the treat with confectioners' sugar, then cut it into squares. Enjoy!

What Games Do We Play?

What do you like to do for fun? Do you like to swim, or ski, or camp? Do you like to read, or draw, or make things?

The **ancient** Greeks enjoyed running races and going to plays. The children of ancient Rome played blindman's buff. The people of Greece and China have been flying kites for more than 2,000 years.

Today, people have fun doing all these things—and more. People skateboard, ski, and snorkel. They watch their favorite sports teams play. They visit zoos, museums, and parks. They play thinking games, and they run, jump, and climb. It's fun to exercise your mind and your body.

On the Playground

Sidewalk games are fun! The names may change, but the games are pretty much the same on playgrounds, sidewalks, and fields all over the world.

Do you play hopscotch? Children all over the world play it. In China, hopscotch is called *Gat Fei Gei,* which means "One-Foot Jumping Flying Machine." In Italy, it's called the *Bell*. In Austria, it's the *Temple*. In Myanmar, children squat with hands on their hips as they jump the squares.

These children in Mexico are playing a game of hopscotch.

Hopscotch games come in all shapes and sizes. Some have 8 squares in a straight line. Others have as many as 20 squares in the shape of a snail's shell.

Hopscotch is a popular sidewalk game all over the world.

80

Outside a monastery in India, children play hopscotch together.

Many children around the world play "Find me, catch me!"

Find Me, Catch Me!

It's Alfredo's turn to be "blind hen." Pedro ties a big, red handkerchief over Alfredo's eyes. Then Pedro, Inez, Maria, and Juan form a circle around Alfredo. The four of them **chant**, "Blind hen, blind hen, what have you lost?"

"I've lost a thimble and a needle," says Alfredo.

"Where have you lost them?" ask the others.

"In a haystack," says Alfredo.

Inez turns Alfredo around three times and steps back. Now the children run up to Alfredo and tease, "Blind hen, blind hen."

Alfredo tries to catch them. But he is confused from being turned around and blindfolded. The children dart away whenever Alfredo's hands come close. Then Juan gets careless—and he is caught. Now it is Juan's turn to be "blind hen."

Alfredo and his friends live in Peru. But "find me, catch me" games like blind hen are played all over the world.

Children in Rome played this game about 2,000 years ago. They called it *murinda*. Nowadays, children in Italy call it *mosca cieca,* "blind fly." In China, it's *tsoo, tsoo.* In Germany, it's *blindekuh.* And in the United States, children call it *blindman's buff.* What do you call it?

Many kinds of games have one person chasing and catching the others. Turn the page to find out how to play!

Catch These Games!

Tired of the same old game of tag? Round up some friends and try these tag games from other countries.

Moon and Morning Stars

The game Moon and Morning Stars comes from Spain. The Moon stands in the shadow of a building or a large tree. He or she must stay in the shadow because the Moon belongs to the night. The other players—Morning Stars—dance in the sunlight but sometimes venture into the shadows and risk being caught. The first star caught becomes the next Moon.

Bow and Curtsy Tag

Try the game Bow and Curtsy Tag—from Sweden. Players stand in a circle, holding hands. The one who is "It" runs around the outside of the circle at least twice, then touches someone's shoulder. The two then run around in opposite directions. When they meet, they stop and bow or curtsy three times. Then they race in opposite directions to take the vacant place in the circle. Whoever loses the race is "It" next time.

Mubwabwa (Antelope)

Here's another fun game, Mubwabwa (Antelope)—from Brazzaville, Congo. Play this game on a field or court with set boundaries. One person is the mubwabwa, or antelope. The mubwabwa tries to catch the others, yelling "Mubwabwa!" Each player who is caught yells "Mubwabwa!" too and helps catch the others. Anyone who goes out of bounds is considered caught. The last person caught is the winner.

Children around the world play many different games with marbles.

Quick Hands, Quick Eyes

This child from Papua New Guinea is turning a string into a cat's cradle. Children all over the world enjoy this tricky game.

In the United States, a game called *jacks* requires quick hands and eyes. Jacks, small metal or plastic pieces, are placed on the floor. A player tries to pick up one or more jacks after tossing, but before catching, a small ball.

Filipino children call the game *siklot*. In India, it is called *guttak*. Instead of jacks, Indian players use small stones.

Can you **crisscross** a string into a cat's cradle? Quick fingers can, in seconds. Within a few more seconds, they can

Girls in India use small stones to play guttak, a game like jacks.

cross the strings again, and another shape appears.

Children everywhere play marbles. In the United States, children play a marbles game called *ringer*. Players use a big marble called a shooter to knock smaller marbles out of a ring.

Pick up sticks is another world favorite. To play, you toss down a fistful of sticks or straws. Then you try to pick up the sticks one by one, without moving any of the others.

Inuit children in Alaska and northern Canada play string games that require quick hands and quick eyes.

Who's First?

Ziggeddy, ziggeddy,
Marble stone,
Pointer, pointer, bouff!
Kisskillindy, kisskillindy,
Pa...Pa...poriff!

That's the rhyme you use to choose who will be "It" in Trinidad, an island in the West Indies. Everyone puts a hand into the circle, and one child says the rhyme while tapping everyone's hand. The child touched on the last word is "It."

Almost every game starts with deciding who goes first. Is it the oldest person, the shortest, or the one with the longest hair? Or do you count around a circle saying "Eeeny, meeny, miny, moe" or "One potato, two potato, three potato, four...."? In Cuba, it's:

> Little white dove,
> Tell me the truth,
> Is it this, or this,
> Or this, forsooth?

In the United States, China, and Japan, children often use the game called *Paper, Scissors, Rock* to decide who goes first. Each player makes a fist. On the count of three, the players throw their fists open, each showing one of the three items. A flat **palm** is paper. Two fingers are scissors. A fist is a rock.

Who wins? Rock beats scissors, by crushing them. Scissors beat paper, by cutting it. Paper beats rock, by covering it.

In Indonesia, the game is called *Elephant, Man, and Ant.* The thumb is an elephant, the first finger is a man, and the little finger is an ant. The elephant can step on the man. The man can scoop up the ant. And the ant can beat the elephant by turning up his trunk and tickling him.

"Elephant," "Man," and "Ant" hand gestures used in Indonesia to pick who's first.

In soccer, known as football in many countries, players try to get a ball into a goal without using their hands.

Good Sports!

People are crowding into the Olympic Stadium in Rome. Banners are flying. Flags are waving. Everyone is talking at once.

The *calcio* (kahl cho) champions from Rome and Milan are about to meet. *Calcio* is the Italian name for soccer. Every Sunday, from October to May, teams from big Italian cities play one another.

"Evviva!" (Hurrah!) A great roar echoes through the stadium as the game begins. Soccer is the favorite sport in Italy, and probably throughout the world. In many

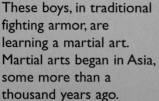

These boys, in traditional fighting armor, are learning a martial art. Martial arts began in Asia, some more than a thousand years ago.

Cricket is a popular sport in England and Australia. In the game, a player hits a ball with a bat.

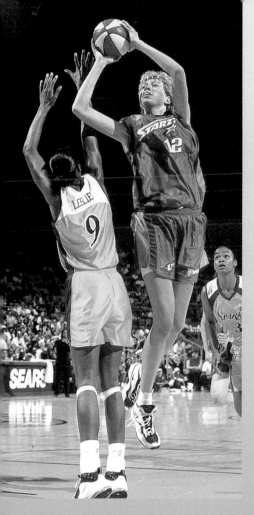

countries in Europe, South America, and Asia, soccer is the national game.

In Canada, ice hockey is the national sport. This game was first played on Canada's frozen lakes and ponds. Now, hockey is popular in western Europe, Russia, the United States, and Japan.

Cricket, the United Kingdom's favorite summer sport, is also popular in Australia, the West Indies, and Pakistan.

Basketball players try to shoot a ball through a hoop. Basketball is popular in many countries.

Americans play all kinds of ball games, such as football, baseball, and basketball. American children love to roller-skate and ride bikes. In Japan, the favorites are volleyball, baseball, and table tennis. Very large wrestlers **compete** in sumo wrestling, another popular sport in Japan.

What's your game?

Don't let the ball drop! In volleyball, players hit a ball back and forth, trying to keep it from hitting the floor on their side of the net.

After an Olympic event, the top three players or teams are honored with a special **ceremony** and medals—gold, silver, and bronze.

First Place!

Do you like to compete? Are you ready to take on the world?

If you are, try the Olympic Games. In the Olympics, athletes representing countries around the world compete for gold, silver, and bronze medals. And the whole world watches.

Do you like archery, fencing, boxing, or rowing? The Olympics have a competition for you. Many sports are

The lighting of the Olympic flame is a **tradition** at the Olympic Games. It stands for spirit, knowledge, life, and peace.

You have to be very strong for the weightlifting competition. Some people lift more than 1,000 pounds (454 kilograms).

included in the Olympic Games. The Winter Olympic Games feature athletes who ski, sled, and skate. The Summer Olympic Games have swimmers, runners, cyclists, jumpers, and gymnasts.

The Olympics have many track and field events. Some are running, but others involve jumping or throwing things.

In some sports, players compete in teams. In others, it's you against your opponent. In some sports, you might race against the clock to beat the record. Ice skaters, divers, and gymnasts all perform before judges who rate their skills.

In sports, someone wins and someone loses. In the Olympic Games, a world-class skier or swimmer might win a medal by only 0.002 second! When you race, you might lose by a hair—or you might win.

Games help you learn to be a good sport—to do your best and enjoy playing, whether you win or lose.

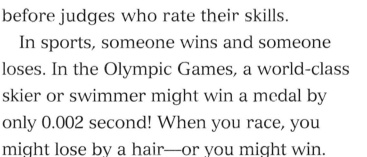

Downhill skiing, or Alpine skiing, can take athletes hurtling down a mountain at speeds of about 60 miles (97 kilometers) per hour.

In-line skating is a fun and active sport. Skaters should always wear protective gear to keep safe.

Hockey is a fun, but fast, sport that should always be played wearing safety equipment.

Playing Safe

Learning to ride a bicycle can be one of the most exciting times in life!

Be prepared like the pros!

Check out the big, tough professional football players. They always wear hard helmets and cover their bodies in safety padding. They are serious about playing it safe.

You should be, too.

Bicycle riding is fun for everyone, and everyone should wear a helmet when they ride.

On paved paths, people love to **glide** on in-line skates and surf on skateboards. Skates and skateboards require balance and speed. A sturdy helmet and a set of wrist, elbow, and kneepads helps keep things safe!

Hockey players of all ages know that helmets, mouthguards, and padding are as important as skates and sticks.

The best surfers and divers have had many swimming lessons. They know you have to be a strong swimmer before you try anything fancy in the water.

Did you know that skateboarding grew out of surfing?

95

Vacation Time

You're on vacation! It's a time to get out and explore. It's a time to try new things and visit different places. It's a time to have fun with your family!

This family is packing their van for a trip.

Some families take trips to faraway places. Other families explore places close to home. City **dwellers** may go to the country. Farmers may head for a big city.

Many families take vacations in summer. During the long summer vacation from school, some children spend time at overnight camps. Others attend day camps, sports camps, or computer camps.

Skiing is a favorite winter sport in the mountains of Japan.

Many French families take summer camping trips. They pitch their tents in campsites operated by the government. These families enjoy the quiet beauty of the forests.

96

This French family is hiking together and enjoying the wilderness.

Winter vacations are fun, too. Japanese families enjoy skiing on the islands of Honshu or Hokkaido. There they race down the snow-covered mountain slopes in the crisp, cold air.

In the United States and Canada, some families vacation at Christmastime, when schools are closed. They often head south to warm places, like Florida, to water ski, sail, or swim.

Where would you like to go on your next vacation? What would you like to do?

What's a Toymaker?

Children all around the world love making toys.

A toymaker is a person who makes toys—a person like you.

Children like you are among the best toymakers in the world. You know toys are as much fun to make as they are to play with. All you need is your imagination and a few **odds and ends.**

A big box can be an ocean liner sailing over the sea or a spaceship landing on the moon.

Bits of cloth and cardboard can be puppets in a play. Pieces of wood float like little boats on puddles and ponds. If you have an old tire, a rope, and a tree, you can make a swing!

This girl in the United States is using cornhusks to make dolls just as her great-grandmother did.

Everywhere, children make toys from things around them. In Bermuda, children make dolls from banana stalks and nuts. In the West African country of Ivory Coast, they make dolls from clumps of grass and roots. In the United States, kids make dolls out of cornhusks.

Mexican children turn cornhusks into toy donkeys. In India, children mold elephants, water buffaloes, and tigers out of clay. In the Solomon Islands, boys use large nuts to make twirling tops.

Do you have some ideas of your own?

All-Time Top Toys

These toys have been pleasing kids for centuries all around the world! Why? Because they are so easy to make and so much fun!

Puppet figures have been found in ancient tombs in Egypt. Shadow puppets are lit behind a screen. Marionettes are puppets controlled by strings. Hands make great puppets too. Slip a sock on your hand and you're ready. Or just draw a face on your fingertip and wiggle it.

A yo-yo is merely two round, flat pieces of wood or plastic joined by a peg and spun on a string, but it has been a favorite for more than 3,000 years! The name yo-yo comes from a Filipino word meaning "come back." Two tricks you can do with a yo-yo are "Walk the Dog," *left,* and "Rock the Baby," *below.*

In 1958, plastic Hula-hoops were first sold in the United States. Ever since then people have been wiggling their hips to keep the hoops rolling around their waists. What other hoop games do you know?

A top can be made of wood, metal, or plastic. Some tops play music as they whirl. You start a top by using a key, by pumping, or with a twist of your fingers or a pull on a string. Children played with tops in ancient Greece.

Toy cars aren't just to be played with. People of all ages collect and make models of cars. Do you have a favorite kind of car you'd like to build a model of?

It bounces higher than a rubber ball. It is very stretchy. It can copy newspaper and comic book words and images. What is it? It's Silly Putty®, and it has been a favorite toy of children since 1949.

Flying disks, more often called Frisbees®, can be thrown a long way. They seem to hover in the air as they fly away from your hand. How far can you throw a Frisbee®?

What is not a living thing but can walk down stairs and steep hills? Why, it's Slinky®. It seems simple, it looks like a coil of wire, but it has fascinated children for many years.

Go Fly a Kite!

As long as there's a steady breeze—and you have a long string—nothing is more fun than flying a kite.

More than 2,000 years ago, someone in China made the very first kite. According to an old story, Chinese soldiers once attached bamboo pipes to kites. As the kites flew over the enemy, wind passed through the pipes. This caused a whistling sound. The enemy soldiers were scared by the noise and ran.

Today children everywhere enjoy flying kites! Hang-glider kites let people soar through the air with a kite. People in India use special kites in the sport of kite fighting.

In Korea, kites serve a happy purpose. Children's wishes for toys are written and tied to kite tails by their mothers. The children fly their kites to tell the gods what they want.

KNOW It All!

Consider some great kite-lovers from history:

Benjamin Franklin did a dangerous experiment in which he attached a metal key to a kite string and flew the kite in a thunderstorm to prove that lightning is electricity. (Don't you do this!)

The Wright brothers used box kites to test their ideas about flight when they were making the first airplane.

Alexander Graham Bell made box kites large enough to lift people off the ground.

People fly colorful kites along the west coast of the United States.

Thinking Caps On!

Care for a challenge? Try using **strategy** in a board game. Derrah is a game like Tic Tac Toe and Go. It is a two-player game from North Africa and is easy to make and fun to play.

What To Do:

1. In Africa, Derrah is played on a wooden board with rows of little round holes, but you can make your own game board. Just trace around a nickel on the paper, drawing six rows of seven circles each. That's 42 circles that form a rectangle, as shown.

2. Decide who goes first. Then set all the pieces on the board, taking turns putting one piece at a time in any empty circle on the board. Only two pieces from the same player can be next to each other.

3. Then take turns moving pieces one space left or right, up or down—but not diagonally. The object is to get three pieces in a row. Choose your moves carefully to try to prevent your opponent from getting three in a row.

4. Each time you get three in a row, you can take one of your opponent's pieces off the board.

The game ends when one player cannot make any more rows of three, or when all of a player's pieces have been taken.

You Will Need:

construction paper

a marker

a nickel

12 matching seeds, stones, buttons, coins, paper clips, or beads for each player

Be sure each players' pieces are different. For example, use white seeds for one and black seeds for another, pennies and dimes, or small and large paper clips.

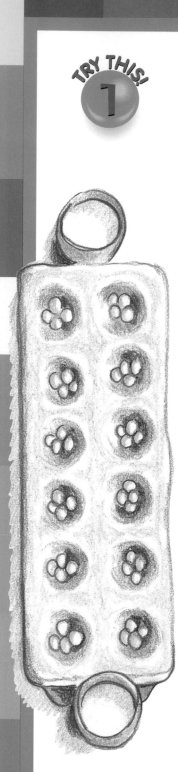

Mancala

Mancala games have been popular in Africa for thousands of years. Two players move small stones or seeds around pits scooped out of a board. The goal is to get the most stones on your side of the board and in your Mancala cup. The trick is deciding which group of stones is best to move!

What To Do:

1. Use an egg carton and two shallow cups for the Mancala board and Mancalas. Each player owns the six pockets on one side of the egg carton and the Mancala cup placed to his or her right.

2. Place four stones in each of the 12 pockets in the egg carton.

3. Decide who will go first. The first player scoops up all the stones from one of his or her six pockets and drops them one by one in the pockets around the carton in a counterclockwise direction starting in the next pocket. If you reach your own Mancala, drop a stone in it, but do not drop stones in your opponent's Mancala.

4. The players will take turns picking up all the stones from a pocket and moving them as described in step three, always taking from one of their own pockets. If the last stone in a turn is placed in the player's own Mancala, the player gets another turn. If the last stone is placed in an empty cup on the player's own side, he or she may take that stone and all the stones from the pocket directly opposite his or her own, if there are any,

108

You Will Need:

an empty egg carton

48 small stones, buttons, marbles, or beads

2 small cups (the Mancalas)

and put them in his or her own Mancala. The game ends when one player's side is clear of stones.

You're the winner if you have more stones in your pockets and Mancala than your opponent does.

People of all ages enjoy playing Mancala together.

How Do We Learn Things?

The world is filled with interesting places to go and fascinating things to know and to do. So where should you go to start learning?

You're already there—wherever you are. You learn at school, at home, at play. You learn from your family and friends and from your teachers. Books and newspapers, television, radio, telephones, and computers offer information from around the world to you.

We are all learning every day. We learn when we listen, we learn when we look, and we learn when we try new things. We're learning when we ask questions and when we try to answer them.

A boy learns to crouch down while hunting in the Kalahari Desert in southern Africa.

Who Teaches You?

Ketwago, a young boy in Botswana (boh TSWAH nah), a small country in Africa, was learning to hunt. Pulling his bowstring tighter, he moved slowly forward. "Stoop as low as you can," said his father from behind him. "When we stoop over, the antelopes think we are animals and they don't run from us. Then you can get close enough to shoot your arrow."

Ketwago doesn't go to school. He is taught by his father and the other

grown-ups of his tribe. Children around the world learn different things in different ways.

Children learn from parents, friends, teachers, librarians, coaches, and brothers and sisters. Everywhere, families teach their children what they think will help them most in their lives.

Students learn a lot of things from their teachers. In this classroom, students are learning about rockets.

A Navajo woman of the American Southwest teaches her granddaughter the way to make rugs and blankets.

These girls in Spain have learned to jump rope. Jumping rope teaches them about how their bodies work.

First Lessons

Little children learn while they play.
Some play in groups at nursery school.
Others visit their friends' houses or play at
home with brothers, sisters, and cousins.

As they play, children teach each other.
They learn how to share and how to listen.
They find out what their bodies can do.
They learn about the world around them.
And they learn how to have fun together.

Four-year-old Carlos lives in Spain.
He plays with his friends, jumping and

climbing in the village. Sometimes they play at one another's homes.

Rohini, a 4-year-old in India, goes to nursery school with her friends. They play with toys, make things, and listen to stories together.

In the United States, 4-year-old Sarah lives on a farm in Iowa. She loves to run and explore in the fields and barn with her older brother.

All children enjoy playing with their friends. And while they play, they are learning from everyone and everything around them.

Children learn how to build shapes with blocks at a nursery school in India.

Education Handed Down

Grown-ups—your parents, teachers, neighbors—teach you many things you need to know in life. They learned these things from the grown-ups they grew up with. People who are even older than your parents, such as your grandparents, older neighbors, great-aunts, and great-uncles, have plenty to teach you, too!

Older grown-ups have a lifetime of experience to share. They have seen the world in many different ways. After all, they started out as children and have been every age between then and now. They were once your age, and they remember how it feels to get a new bike, have a baby brother or sister, or go to school. They may have helpful answers to your problems and funny stories to tell.

All older grown-ups have special skills. Their jobs and their skills are things they can teach you. Maybe your grandfather knows all about fishing. Maybe an older neighbor knows a lot about gardening. Maybe they speak another language or once lived in another country. You can learn a lot from them.

TRY THIS! 1

The older grown-ups in your life were once exactly your age. Where did they live? What chores did they do? What games did they play? What books did they read? Ask them! Find out how their childhood was like your own, and how it was different.

Where Do You Go to School?

This temple in Thailand becomes a school for the village children.

Do you go to school in a classroom with lots of desks and chairs or at your kitchen table? In a temple or in a one-room schoolhouse? Do you go to school indoors or outdoors?

A school may be any kind of building, or it may not be a building at all! A school is simply a place where students come to learn with help from a teacher. All around the world, children go to schools of all kinds and all sizes to learn the things they need to know.

In Kashmir, India, children may gather on the ground outside to listen to a teacher and learn.

This girl is learning computer skills in a classroom in Australia.

These children in Peru are listening to their teacher in a classroom.

These children in Colombia paddle canoes to get to a school that stands on stilts.

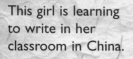
This girl is learning to write in her classroom in China.

120

Home-schooled children in the United States and around the world take lessons from their parents at home.

At this village school in the Middle East, students sit on rugs on the floor.

In many places throughout the world, children sit at desks in classrooms to learn. These British children are working on a writing assignment.

Barge children study as they travel. They go to classes in the cities and towns along the waterways.

Traveling Schools

Do you go to the same school every day? Some children don't. They go to lots of different schools, and some days they don't go to school at all!

These children live with their families on boats called **barges**. The barges are always on the move. They travel up and down rivers and canals in the Netherlands, France, and Germany, carrying goods from one town to another.

In the Netherlands, barge children go to special schools in the towns where the barges stop. While the barges are tied up, the children attend classes. They are also given lessons to work on as they travel.

When the barge gets to the next stop, the children go to another school. They hand in their homework, go to classes, and get more homework to do. In this way, they can keep up with their schoolwork.

When these barge children finish their elementary schooling, they may go to live with a family on shore. Then they can go to a regular high school.

In school, children learn how to study and how to find out things they want to know.

You're Learning

Everywhere you look there are exciting things to do, new things to try! At school, your teachers are introducing you to a world of ideas. They also are giving you the tools you need to explore that world. In school and out of school, children find new things they want to learn. They are having fun learning skills they will enjoy all their lives.

Children may paint, draw, and learn all kinds of crafts at school. These Indian children are enjoying a craft lesson in the sun.

This boy is finishing a cat sculpture in his art class.

These students are learning about plants from their teacher.

These children are using microscopes, which make things look much larger than they are. Can you think of things you'd like to see this way?

Special Skills

Akibo kneels on a rooftop. He puts down his bundle of **thatch** and ties it in place. Akibo works carefully. He wants to be the best student in his class.

Akibo lives in Malawi (mah LAH wee), a small country in southern Africa. He and his classmates are learning how to build a house. The boys learn how to make a thatched roof. The girls learn how to mix clay and water to make mud and plaster it over branches to make the walls.

In Iran, Omar lives and works in the home of a master **weaver.** His town, Kerman, is known for its beautiful Persian rugs. Every day, Omar weaves carpets and learns more about his craft.

Children need to know a lot besides how to read, write, and do arithmetic. They also need to learn things that are important in their **culture.** Children everywhere learn skills that will be useful when they grow up.

In the United States, many young people learn how to use the kitchen stove, so they can help prepare meals. They also learn how to read maps to find places and how to use a library to find out many things.

In Morocco, some children learn how to spin and dye wool for carpets. This boy is hanging out dyed wool to dry in the sun.

Children from Mali in Africa, *upper right,* take part in building a hut. The skills they are learning will be needed when they are grown up. A child in the United States, *lower right,* learns to read a map.

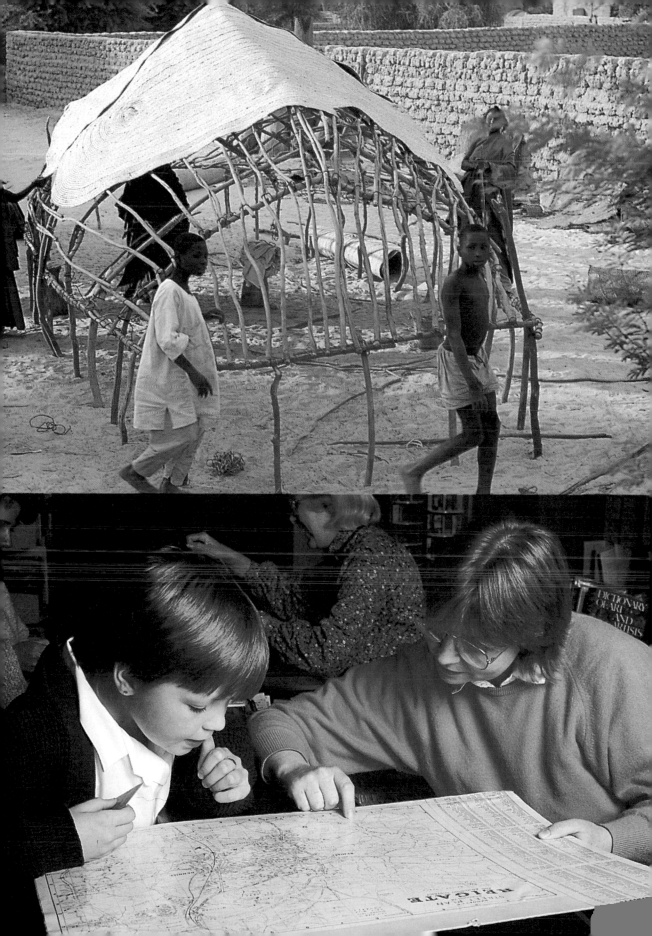

When people who do not speak the same language get together, they talk through interpreters.

Many Languages

How many ways can you say "Hello"? Some children speak more than one language, because the people they live with speak different languages. Children who live in places like Western Europe, where many countries and cultures are close together, often learn a second language.

Even people who speak the same language don't always say words the same way. In the United States, people in

The same word spoken in different ways can have different meanings in Chinese.

mother

horse

scold

Canada has two official languages, English and French. Many children there learn to speak both.

the northeastern states may say "dahg." People in the southeastern states may say "dawg." They are all saying the word *dog,* but they have different ways of saying it.

There are about 6,000 languages in the world, and most people speak and understand only one or two. People who know more than one language can become interpreters. Interpreters are people who translate words from one language into another. When world leaders meet, they often exchange ideas through an interpreter.

TRANS CANADA

2

N. B.

WEST
OUEST

Hello, Olá, Hola

How many different ways can you say *hello*?
Here are seven different ways. Try them!

In French, you say *Bon jour*
In Portuguese, you say *Olá*
In Turkish, you say *Merhaba*
In Vietnamese, you say *Xin Chào*
In Spanish, you say *Hola*
In Lithuanian, you say *Labas*
In Swahili, you say *Jambo*

Now, how do you "see" hello? It depends on who's writing it! Try your hand at some of these friendly written greetings from around the world:

今日は
kon
nichi
wa

Japanese

你好嗎
nai
hao
ma

Chinese

ЗДРАВСТВУЙТЕ
Zdrav st voo ee tee eh

Russian

שלום
shalom

Hebrew

நமஸ்காரம்
na ma s ka ra m

Tamal—Sri Lanka

زياك صحة
zayak sahha

Arabic

नमस्ते
na ma stè

Hindi—India

Do you want to learn more words in another language? Find a radio station or TV channel on which people are speaking another language. Listen for a while. See if you can figure out what some of the words mean. Practice saying them. Or read product labels and public signs that include your language and another language. Compare the words and see what you can figure out.

131

Armenian children say:
Meg, yergoo, yergunnas;
Yerec, chors, choranas;
Hinc, vets, vernas;
Yoten, ooten, ooranas;
Innin, dacenin, jam yertas;
Dacen, dasnergu, hats geran.

...which means this in English:
One, two, grow tall;
Three, four, round as a ball;
Five, six, reach up high;
Seven, eight, don't scratch the sky;
Nine, ten, time for mass;
Eleven, twelve, lunch at last.

132

One, Two, Buckle My Shoe

Children everywhere learn counting rhymes—but not the same ones. Try saying these counting rhymes from different countries. Don't worry about saying the words exactly right. Just try sounding them out the way you would an English word. The one on this page rhymes in its original language, but not in English.

In Germany, children say:
Eins, zwei, Polizei;
Drei, vier, Offizier;
Fünf, sechs, alte Hex;
Sieben, acht, gute Nacht.
Neun, zehn, Capitän;
Elf, zwölf, einige Wölf.

...which means this in English:
One, two, police;
Three, four, officer;
Five, six, old witch;
Seven, eight, good night.
Nine, ten, captain;
Eleven, twelve, some wolves.

Body Language

Did you stick out your tongue? In Tibet, you're saying, "I respect you." In North America, you're saying just the opposite!

Did you tap your forehead? In the United States, you are saying "smart." In the Netherlands, you are saying "crazy."

Every day, you use your arms and hands and head or other parts of your body to help you say things. Sometimes your actions say things almost better than words can.

In school, you raise your hand. This tells the teacher you are asking for a turn to speak. When riding a bicycle, you let others know you are going to turn by signaling with your arm. Once in a while, you might shrug your shoulders to tell someone, "I don't know," or "Hmmm, maybe."

Babies are body language pros. They fuss, laugh, and snuggle. Their mothers and fathers respond to every "word."

Everyone around the world uses body language to speak. We all greet a friend with a smile, and we all frown or cry when we are sad. But be careful! Some body language means different things in different places.

A mountain tribesman in Nigeria claps his hands to show respect and to say, "Thank you."

In Japan, people bow when they meet.

TRY THIS!
1

Look at the comic strips in the newspaper. Cartoonists, the people who draw cartoons, know how to let faces do the talking. The eyebrows, eyes, and mouths tell you how the characters feel. Use some of the expressions here to create drawings of your own!

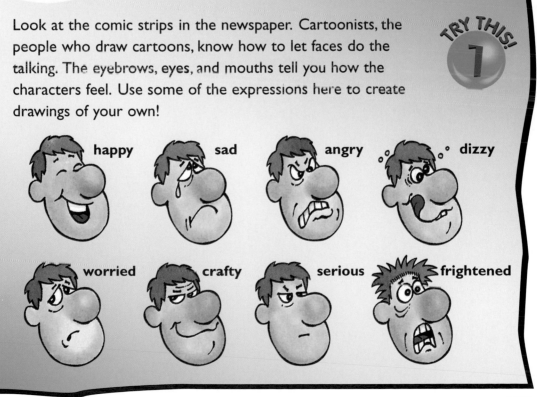

happy   sad   angry   dizzy

worried   crafty   serious   frightened

These clowns say, "That's a very smelly little skunk!"

This signal is very clear. "Go that way," says a traffic policeman in Fiji.

136

Did someone tell you "Shhh"? In the United States, you need to be quiet. In Germany, you'd better "hurry up."

Saying good-bye? Wave to North Americans with your **palm** facing out, fingers waving. Wave to Italians or Peruvians with your palm facing in.

Did you nod your head, then shake your head? In most countries, you said "Yes," then "No." In Bulgaria, you said "No," then "Yes."

Are you making a circle with your forefinger and thumb? In most countries, that means "Okay!" In France, it means "It's worthless." In Greece and Italy, it's an insult.

Want to point to something? In most countries, you use your finger. In Thailand, you use your chin.

A pinch on the cheek is a friendly greeting and a sign of affection in some parts of Eastern Europe.

Sign Here

Baseball teams have their own secret hand signs. A coach on the sideline may touch his hat, pat his knee, or rub his nose to send a message to a player on the field.

People who are deaf use sign language every day. They use their hands and faces to make signs that stand for words or ideas. They also spell out words by shaping letters with their fingers.

You probably already know a few signs yourself. How do you say "Good-bye," "Okay," and "Stop!" without making a sound? What other signs do you use or see?

KNOW It All!

People who are deaf and blind can learn to feel what people say if words are finger-spelled into their hands.

Native American Hand Signs

For many years, Native American tribes with different languages used hand signs to talk and trade together. These pictures show some of the signs they used. Try them by yourself or with a friend!

"Father"—Touch the right side of your chest several times with your right fist.

"Mother"—Touch the left side of your chest several times with your right fist.

father

"I"—Point to yourself with your right thumb. For the sign "You," point to the other person with your right thumb.

I

"Thank you"—Hold your hands chest high, palms facing out. Push your hands slowly toward the person you wish to thank, letting your hands curve downward.

thank you

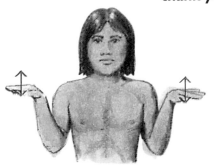

"Bird"—Hold your hands at your shoulders. Move your hands up and down, like the flapping of a bird's wings.

bird

American Sign Language

In American Sign Language, you can make symbols for every letter of the alphabet using your right hand. You can also learn hand movements for words.

1. Practice making the letters of the alphabet shown here. Then learn to spell out your own name using sign language.

2. Here are some common signs. Ask your friends and family to guess what you're signing.

Good   **Night**   **Tree**   **Moon**

A giant paintbrush shows everyone what this store in Guatemala sells.

Signs and Symbols

Today, a plane can take you quickly to any place in the world. But, what if you don't speak the language of the people there? Don't worry. Countries around the world use picture signs.

In Afghanistan, some roads are for cars and trucks and others are for camels and

This Arabic sign tells about a mystery movie that's showing in Cairo, Egypt.

donkeys. Drivers from other countries can tell which road is which by picture signs. Almost anyone can understand where to go.

Signs with simple drawings of cars, people, and objects instead of words are easy to "read" even if you can't read at all.

Can you guess what people buy at this butcher shop in France?

This picture sign in Afghanistan shows truck drivers and camel drivers which roads to take.

143

This sign warns cars to slow down because they are near a playground.

Drivers know they are near a crosswalk when they see this sign.

"Caution! This is a bicycle crossing," warns this sign in France.

You read picture signs every day. What do a fork, knife, and spoon on a road sign mean? What does a bed on a sign mean? Have you seen animal-crossing signs for deer, horses, or cows? What is the symbol for a school crossing?

How do signs say "School Zone," or "Deer Crossing"? What signs tell you that restrooms and telephones are nearby? Do you know the sign for a playground? The sign for a library?

144

Watch out! Your car will end up in the water if you don't stop when you see this warning sign.

KIDS ONLY!

TRY THIS!

7

Make up some picture signs of your own. What sign can you make and put on your bedroom door or the kitchen table?

145

Beating Out Messages

A tribesman from Tanzania beats out a message on a wooden drum.

"Listen!"

The men stopped and stood very still. The air was filled with sounds—birds screeching, monkeys chattering—the usual jungle noises.

There it was again—drumbeats sounding clear above the din of the jungle. They listened until the sound stopped.

"Come," one man said, "We are needed at the village."

How did he know that? By listening to a "jungle telegram." In Tanzania (TAN zuh NEE uh) and other countries in Africa, drums called *gongos* are still used to send messages.

A gongo is a big, hollow log with a long slot in it. If you beat on one side of the slot, it makes a low note. If you beat on the other side, it makes a high note. These two notes make up gongo language.

Drum messages take a long time. Even a short word like *dog* may require as many as 14 drumbeats. And all messages are sent twice.

Every village has a gongo and every gongo has a name. The name of the gongo is beaten out before or after a message to identify the sender. The gongo at one village is called "Master of the river." A nearby gongo is named "The evil spirit has no friend or kin."

This little girl is reading the newspaper with her father. He helps her with words she doesn't know yet.

What's the News?

"Read all about it!" the **newsvendor** cries. He knows people want the latest news.

What happened yesterday? Who won the big game? Will it rain tomorrow? People everywhere are curious about events both near and far.

Most people buy newspapers to read at home or while on a train or bus. In some places, newspapers arc tacked up on walls so people passing by can read the news. People who can't read listen as others read the newspaper out loud.

In Chinese cities, newspapers are pinned up outside so that anyone can stop and read them.

Some newspapers present news on events happening all over the world. Other newspapers print stories about only one neighborhood or area.

Millions of newspapers are printed every day throughout the world. Nearly every country has at least one daily paper. In many big countries, hundreds of different newspapers are printed and read every day.

Some newspapers have many pages and are printed on huge printing presses. Other newspapers have only a single page and are printed on small copying machines. Some little newspapers are even written by hand.

People can send letters, computer files, and other kinds of information from one computer to another using electronic mail, or e-mail.

KNOW It All!!

For up-to-the-minute news any time of day or night, people turn on their computers. On the World Wide Web, part of the Internet, electronic newspapers keep people up on the very latest news.

News Right Now

You can get up-to-the-minute news of the world at the flip of a switch. Electronic machines such as televisions, radios, telephones, teletext, and computers put the news at your fingertips.

You can even watch news as it happens, all around the world. Television signals bounce off objects called **artificial satellites** out in space. The satellites send TV **broadcasts** from station to station, anywhere on the earth.

Teletext is another up-to-the-minute news source. With teletext, people can receive the latest news as printed information and pictures on their television screens.

Telephone conversations bounce off space satellites or travel through cables lying on the ocean floor so that people on opposite sides of the world can talk to each other.

Using a computer with a modem, the part that connects to phone wires, you can get news from the World Wide Web on the **Internet**. And you can send and receive news using electronic mail.

These Polynesians are sitting on grass mats to watch television. Their home is open to the warm tropical breezes.

A cell phone, a phone with no wires, helps this man call for help when his car breaks down.

How Do We All Get Along?

More than 6 billion people call our planet home. There are thousands of different languages and many different religions. In a world so full of people and ideas, how do we all get along?

Friends and neighbors have **customs** that tell them how to behave. Customs are the "manners" of a country or group of people.

Families and schools have rules about how people should treat one another. The rules spell out what is fair to all.

Countries have laws that tell people what they can and cannot do. Laws show us how to treat other people and our planet with respect.

How should you treat someone from another country? Follow the laws and the rules where you are and respect the local customs. When everyone works together, people get along.

We should eat nicely
so we don't bother
others at the table.

What Is Etiquette?

Do you like it when people:

Let you finish what you are saying?

Hold a door open for you?

Help you carry a heavy load?

Let you join their game?

Children learn from grown-ups, such as parents and teachers, wherever they

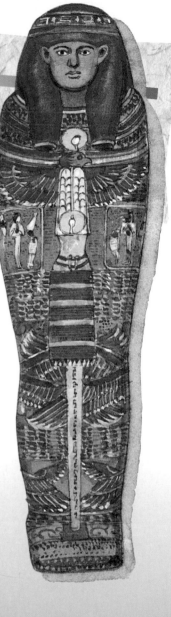

KNOW It All!

The first known guide to etiquette was written by a government official in **ancient** Egypt around 2400 B.C.

go. They learn how to behave at dinner, in school, and for different situations. For example, they learn to sit up straight. They learn to use a napkin when eating. Why do you think it's good manners not to talk with food in your mouth?

It is almost always proper etiquette (EHT ih keht) to say "please" when you ask for something or need help. For example, if you ask a librarian for help finding a book, you say "please."

When you receive something, you say "thank you" to show you appreciate what you got. It also is good manners to thank people for giving you information.

When you say "excuse me," you're telling those near you that you didn't mean any harm or that you didn't do something on purpose. For example, when you get

155

Etiquette can be tricky. Sometimes, what is polite in one country might be rude in another. In Japan, you should take off your shoes when you enter a house. In the United States, guests usually keep their shoes on.

off a crowded elevator or bus, you say "excuse me" if you bump someone.

A tricky part of good manners includes changing your speech to fit the occasion. It would be silly and not very helpful to call, "Excuse me, please, but I'll catch that for you" when you are playing baseball. By the time you finished talking, the ball would be on the ground! Ball-playing etiquette requires you to say, quickly and clearly, "Mine!" when you are catching a fly ball.

In North America, it is polite to shake hands when meeting. In Japan, you should bow slightly to say hello.

What's the right thing to do? If you don't know, ask someone. One way to get it "right" most of the time is to act the way you would like others to behave.

If we bump someone, we should say, "Excuse me."

TRY THIS!
1

Magic Words

What magic words should each of these people use? Choose "please," "excuse me," or "thank you."

See answers on page 159.

1. Is that for me?
_____.

2. _____, I didn't mean to bump you.

3. _____ , Mom, but I have something to tell you.

4. Would you help me up, _____.

5. _____ for the
tickets.

6. _____ for
helping me.

7. _____ for
the gift.

8. Would you
_____ fix
this for me.

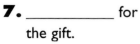

We should wait politely for our turn to drink.

Wait Your Turn

Tom was visiting his cousin Colin in London, England. It was Saturday. The boys were on their way to the Tower of London to see the Crown Jewels.

At the bus stop, Colin got in line behind the other people. Tom thought this was strange. In New York City, he was used to people standing around any which way until the bus came.

"Is there a law here that tells people to stand in line to wait for a bus?" Tom asked.

"Of course not," replied Colin. "But to

tell the truth, I never thought about it before. We always stand in line. It's called queuing (KYOO ing) up. People started waiting that way because it was the polite way to do it. Today, it's a custom." When people behave in a certain way for a long time, this way of doing things often becomes a custom. Customs are not the same everywhere. In some places, a custom is as important as a law.

Queuing up is not a law. But British people do it because they feel it makes life easier for everyone.

These people are "queuing up" for a bus in York, England.

This boy is taking his daily bath at the well, while his sister polishes a pair of shoes.

This young girl in Peru is bringing home a bundle of firewood. She must do this task every day.

TRY THIS!
1
What are five rules at your house? What other rules would you make?

Do I Have To?

"Aw, come on! Let's play one more game."

"We can't. We have to go home now."

David and Franny didn't want to stop playing, but it was almost dinnertime. If they didn't leave now, they'd be late. Being on time for dinner is a rule in their family. There are other rules, too—rules about bedtime, rules about safety, rules about being polite.

Sometimes David forgets to turn off lights or complains about washing his hands before meals. Franny sometimes puts off picking up her belongings, and she hates going to bed first just because she's younger.

But both children know that family rules are important. By doing what's expected of them, children help the whole family.

Rules aren't just for children, of course. Adults have rules they must follow every day, too. The rules they follow help them. Grown-ups have many tasks they do to take good care of their families and their homes.

For example, grown-ups must earn money to buy the family what it needs. They also must make sure the family is fed.

At dinnertime, this girl helps set the table.

Each morning this boy makes his bed.

In Mauritania, some people have village meetings to make decisions about laws.

It's the Law!

Every family has rules. Some rules are made by parents and children together. Other rules are made by the parents alone. Once they are set, family rules must be followed.

Rules help the members of a family live happily together. If you break a family rule, what happens? Maybe you have to do extra work as a punishment. Maybe you are "grounded" for a while.

Laws are the rules that help the people in a community—or a whole country—live peacefully together. The laws of a town, country, or tribe must be obeyed by all of the people there.

Who makes the laws? In a tribe, it may be the chief and a council of tribal members. In some small towns, most or all of the adults gather together to make laws. In large cities and countries, a few people make the laws for everyone.

What laws do you know? Do you have a favorite law? What law would you make if you were a leader in your community?

Police officers try to make sure people obey a country's laws.

TRY THIS!
1

Laws affect everyone—even family pets. If you are a pet owner, find out what the local laws are for cats, dogs, horses, or other animals you have. For example, some places have a leash law, which means you must walk your dog on a leash. Are registration tags needed? What shots are required? Can you keep a wild animal in your yard?

You may also want to ask a police officer about your local bicycle laws. Does your bike need to be registered? What lights, reflectors, and bells or horns does it need? Are riders required to wear helmets?

Sharing the Work

Sharing the work means sharing the fun.

People don't just follow laws and rules. They have responsibilities or jobs, too. By doing these jobs, they help each other and themselves.

In some families, adults and children work side by side every day, planting, tending, and harvesting crops in the fields. In other families, everyone helps sell goods in a small store or on the street.

This girl is pitching in at school by helping to water the plants.

These Guatemalan families sell fresh fruit, vegetables, and flowers on the street.

Everyone pitches in at harvest time on a German farm.

Families do different kinds of work in different places. But, in every family, grown-ups and children help one another. When everybody helps, the work gets done more quickly. And, everyone can share pride in a job well done.

Most children have jobs to do at home, too. Some take out the garbage or recycling, put away the laundry, or feed the family pet. Some children help take care of their younger brothers and sisters. Maybe you set the table or wash the dishes.

As you do your share of the family's work, you are learning to be responsible and to help others. What jobs, or responsibilities, do you have at home?

Bath Time for Buffaloes

How would you like to ride a water buffalo?

Water buffaloes really do love water. In Asia, people use these huge animals to plow fields and rice paddies. Buffaloes are work animals, not pets. Still, children enjoy caring for them—especially when it's bath time!

After working hard in the sun, buffaloes need a rest. During the hottest part of the day, children ride them to the nearest lake or river. Here, the buffaloes sink happily into the water. They love to wallow in the soft, cool mud with only their eyes and noses showing. The children splash and swim around while the animals cool off. Then, they give the buffaloes a good scrub. After such a nice break, the buffaloes are ready to go on with the day's work.

Inuit children in Northern Canada help train sled dogs. At stables in the United Kingdom, children may groom horses. On farms around the world, children feed chickens and ducks.

Do you walk your dog or feed your cat? Do you fill the feeder for the birds outside? If you do, you're helping animals too.

It's fun to take care of animals—whether they are work animals, pets, or wildlife near our homes.

Putting food out for birds during colder weather is an easy way to help animals.

These Inuit children in Alaska are caring for and playing with puppies that will grow up to be sled dogs.

All Together Now

You're lined up at the curb to watch the parade. Here comes the marching band! They step in time and make exciting music together.

But look closely. Each band member is doing something different. The drummer and the clarinet, trumpet, and tuba players are all playing different parts of the music. Alone, they sound good, but when they all play together— they sound wonderful!

Now look at your neighbors who are watching the parade. They all work together to make your community a good place to live. Each person has important responsibilities to the community. Their jobs help make the community a nice place for everyone to live.

From the people who make traffic laws to the police officers who enforce them and the drivers who obey them— everyone works together to make your streets safe.

From the people who **recycle** trash to the workers who handle it and the companies who use the materials again—everyone works together to protect our resources.

You help your community, too. When you welcome a new neighbor, plant flowers, or clean up a vacant lot, you're doing your part to make the community a nice place to live. Can you think of other ways you help the community?

Musicians in marching bands play together to bring lively music to a parade.

171

Team Up

In a tug of war, many little children pulling together can win the game. They might even drag a grown-up through the mud!

The people on a rowing team must work together, too. If the rowers all pulled their oars when they felt like it, the boat would never get anywhere, much less win a race.

Rowing teams—like many other teams— have a leader. A rowing-team leader is called a coxswain. The coxswain steers the boat and calls out the timing to the closest rower. This rower sets the pace so that all the rowers pull at the same time.

People often work together to get a job done. Most of the time, they choose a leader. Then they decide on a plan of action. The leader directs the work of the group and makes sure each person does part of the work.

Even animals know how to "team up" for success. In the frozen lands of Alaska and northern Canada, sled-dog teams run as one. All the dogs follow the lead dog as they pull the sled and driver across the snow.

Divide a group into teams with at least three people on each team. Place two identical plastic cups on a line in front of the teams and a bucket of water behind each team. Give each team a tablespoon. Set a timer for two minutes. During the two minutes, team members on each team take turns carrying a spoonful of water from the bucket to the plastic cup. The team that has the most water in its cup after two minutes wins the game.

The Turnip

Once upon a time an old man planted a little turnip and said: "Grow, grow, little turnip, grow sweet! Grow, grow, little turnip, grow strong!"

And the turnip grew up sweet and strong and big and enormous.

Then, one day, the old man went to pull it up. He pulled and pulled again, but he could not pull it up.

He called the old woman.

The old woman pulled the old man, the old man pulled the turnip.

And they pulled and pulled again, but they could not pull it up.

So the old woman called her granddaughter.

The granddaughter pulled the old woman,
The old woman pulled the old man,
The old man pulled the turnip.

And they pulled and pulled again, but they could not pull it up.

The granddaughter called the dog.
The dog pulled the granddaughter,
The granddaughter pulled the old woman,
The old woman pulled the old man,
The old man pulled the turnip.

And they pulled and pulled again,
but they could not pull it up.
The dog called the cat.
The cat pulled the dog,
The dog pulled the granddaughter,
The granddaughter pulled the old woman,
The old woman pulled the old man,
The old man pulled the turnip.
And they pulled and pulled again,
but still they could not pull it up.

The cat called the mouse.
The mouse pulled the cat,
The cat pulled the dog,
The dog pulled the granddaughter,
The granddaughter pulled the old woman,
The old woman pulled the old man,
The old man pulled the turnip.
They pulled and pulled again, and up
came the turnip at last.

People in many countries vote to select the leaders of their country.

Who's in Charge?

At school, it's the principal. On a baseball team, it's the coach. In an army, it's the general. These people are leaders and it's their job to run things.

Countries are run by leaders too. Different countries have different kinds of leaders.

Some leaders are elected by the people of the country. That means the people vote for their leader. They elect a president, prime minister, or premier. Canada, France, India, Mexico, and the United States all have elected leaders.

In some countries, the leader is a king or queen. Kings and queens are not chosen by the people. They are members of the country's royal family. When the king or queen dies, another royal family member takes over. Saudi Arabia and Swaziland (SWAH zee land) have ruling kings.

Some countries have both a king or queen and an elected leader. The Netherlands, Norway, Sweden, and the United Kingdom have queens or kings, but the real leaders of these countries are prime ministers elected by the people.

Some countries have leaders who are chosen—or choose themselves—for life. Only when they die will a new leader take charge.

This queen is traveling in her carriage after an important political event.

This Moroccan king waves to his people after leading them in a prayer.

179

No Place to Live

Your home may be a palace, an apartment, a farmhouse, a houseboat, or a trailer. It is the place where you feel safe, warm, and loved.

But not everyone has a home. Millions of people in the world are homeless. They live in the open and sleep under bridges, in **refugee** camps, even in open fields.

Sometimes, people lose their homes. Natural disasters like floods, earthquakes, and hurricanes can wipe out entire neighborhoods or villages and leave many families homeless.

People also lose their homes when they flee from a war or when they are starving and must find food elsewhere. Some people become homeless because they can't find work or a low-cost place to live.

Children whose families are homeless must sometimes spend their childhood working, rather than playing games or going to school.

Fortunately, many people help the homeless. When there are natural

This volunteer is helping a homeless man find a coat and gloves to keep him warm.

disasters, people and groups from all over the world send money, food, and medical supplies. Governments often help people who must flee a war.

Cities have **shelters** where people can sleep and be safe. Charities provide meals and warm clothing. Some groups build houses for the homeless, and others offer job training.

Ask a grown-up what you can do to help the homeless in your community.

Sharing One World

All children should have food to eat, a safe place to live, good medical care, and an education. These are called rights. A family helps protect its children's rights.

The biggest "family" in the world is the United Nations, or UN for short. The UN makes rules to protect the rights of everyone in the world's family. If people somewhere are being mistreated or denied food, safety, shelter, or freedom, the UN can step in to help them.

The UN members include nearly every country. At the UN **headquarters** in New York City, leaders from those countries work together to keep peace in the world.

The world family plays together too. Athletes from around the world **compete** in sports at the Olympic Games every two years. The winter games happen one year, and then, two years later, it's time for the summer games.

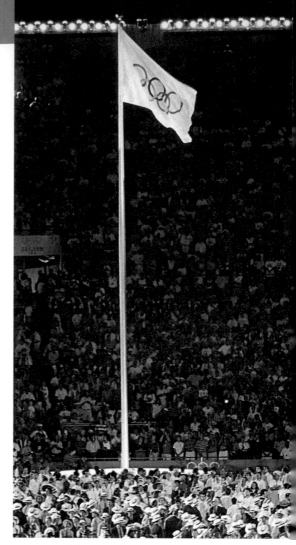

During the opening **ceremony** of the Olympic Games, people from many countries **celebrate** together.

At a United Nations meeting, people from around the world talk about how to keep peace in the world.

The world is filled with different races, different religions, and different ways of life. When the different people get together to solve problems or play sports, they learn to respect each other, help each other, and be friends.

The world's children have their own ways of getting together. International groups like the Boy Scouts, Girl Scouts, and Girl Guides help children from around the world meet and have fun.

Glossary

Here are some of the words you read in this book. Many of them may be new to you. Some are hard to pronounce. But since you will see them again, they are good words to know. Next to each word, you will see how to say it correctly: **ballerina** (BAL uh REE nuh). The part shown in small capital letters is said a little more loudly than the rest of the word. The part in large capital letters is said the loudest. Under each word are one or two sentences that tell what the word means.

A

aborigines (AB uh RIJ uh neez)
Aborigines are the earliest known people to live in a place, such as the first Australians.

ancient (AYN shuhnt)
Something that is ancient is from long ago.

artificial satellite (ahr tuh FIHSH uhl SAT uh lyt)
An artificial satellite is a manufactured object that is launched into space to orbit the earth and send signals from one place to another.

B

barge (bahrj)
A barge is a large, flat-bottomed boat used to carry goods up and down rivers.

broadcast (BRAWD kast)
A broadcast is a news or entertainment program on radio or television.

C

celebrate (SEHL uh brayt)
To celebrate is to mark an important day or event with special activities.

ceremony (SEHR uh MOH nee)
A ceremony consists of formal actions or words used to mark a special occasion.

chant (chant)
To chant is to say or sing the same words again and again.

Christians (KRIHS chuhnz)
Christians are people who follow the teachings of Jesus Christ.

coming of age (KUHM ihng uhv AYJ)
The time when a teen-ager is first becoming an adult is called his or her coming of age.

compete (kuhm PEET)
To compete is to try to win. Many people enjoy competing in sports.

crisscross (KRIHS kraws)
To crisscross something is to make lines back and forth across each other.

culture (KUHL chuhr)
The customs, arts, laws, and beliefs of a group of people at a certain time in history is its culture.

custom (KUHS tuhm)
A custom is the way a group of people has done something for a long time. Every country has customs.

D

disgust (dihs GUHST)
Disgust is a strong dislike for something.

dweller (DWEHL uhr)
A person who lives or makes a home in a place is called a dweller. A person who lives in a forest is a forest dweller.

E

embroidery (ehm BROY duhr ee)
Embroidery is a colorful design sewn on cloth with needle and thread.

F

folk costume (fohk KAHS toom)
The traditional clothing worn by the people of a country or a region is called a folk costume.

G

glide (glyd)
To glide is to move along smoothly with little or no effort.

grain (grayn)
Grain is the seed part of such cereal plants as wheat, corn, or rice.

H

headquarters (HEHD kwawr tuhrz)
Headquarters are the main offices of a business or group.

Hindu (HIHN doo)
A Hindu is a person who follows Hinduism, the major religion of India.

I

Internet (IHN tuhr neht)
The Internet is a worldwide network of computers.

Inuit (IHN yoo iht)
The Inuit are a people who live in and near the Arctic, including in Alaska, Canada, and Greenland.

K

kibbutz (kih BUHTZ)
A kibbutz is a farming community in Israel in which everyone shares the work. The children in a kibbutz may live separately from the grown-ups.

N

newsvendor (NOOZ VEHN duhr)
A newsvendor is a person who sells newspapers.

O

odds and ends (ahdz and ehndz)
Leftover items, scraps, and one-of-a-kind things are sometimes called odds and ends.

P

palm (pahm)
The flat inner part of your hand between the fingers and the wrist is called your palm.

pickled (PIHK uhld)
A vegetable that has been soaked in salt water or vinegar has been pickled. The most common pickled vegetables are cucumbers.

R

recycle (ree SY kuhl)
To recycle is to reuse something or to change or treat waste material so that it can be used again. Many people recycle newspaper, aluminum cans, and glass.

refugee (ref yuh JEE)
A refugee is a person who flees to a place of safety or shelter from some danger or trouble. A refugee camp is a place where refugees can stay.

S

shellfish (SHEHL fihsh)
Animals that have hard outer coverings and live in water are called shellfish. Clams, lobsters, and crabs are all shellfish.

shelter (SHEHL tuhr)
Shelter is a structure that covers or protects. A house is a shelter.

simmer (SIHM uhr)
To simmer is to boil gently.

strategy (strat UH gee)
A strategy is a plan for solving a problem or winning a game.

T

thatch (thach)
The straw, leaves, or other similar material used to cover a roof is called thatch.

thrive (thryv)
To thrive is to grow in a lively, successful way.

traditions (truh DIHSH uhnz)
Traditions are customs and beliefs handed down through generations.

W

weaver (WEEV uhr)
A weaver is a person who passes threads or strips of material over and under each other in a crisscross pattern to make rugs, baskets, or cloth.

worship (WUR shihp)
To worship is to pray to God or another holy being.

Y

yeast (yeest)
Yeast is a substance used in baking to make dough rise.

Index

This index is an alphabetical list of important topics covered in this book. It will help you find information given in both words and pictures. To help you understand what an entry means, there is sometimes a helping word in parentheses, for example, **Aborigines** (people). If there is information in both words and pictures, you will see the words *with pictures* in parentheses after the page number. If there is only a picture, you will see the word *picture* in parentheses after the page number.

188

Illustration Acknowledgments

The Publishers of *Childcraft* gratefully acknowledge the courtesy of the following illustrators, photographers, agencies, and organizations for illustrations in this volume. When all the illustrations for a sequence of pages are from a single source, the inclusive page numbers are given. Credits should be read from top to bottom, left to right, on their respective pages. All illustrations are the exclusive property of the publishers of *Childcraft* unless names are marked with an asterisk (*).

Cover — Children with cardboard faces—© Ed Honowitz, Tony Stone Images*; Girl playing hopscotch—Eileen Mueller Neill; Child eating noodles—International Society for Educational Information, Tokyo, Inc.*; Girl with Hula hoop—© Kransco*

Back Cover — International Society for Educational Information, Tokyo, Inc.*

1 — Eileen Mueller Neill; International Society for Educational Information, Tokyo, Inc.*; © Kransco*

2-3 — Nan Brooks; Joan Holub; Rick Incrocci

4-5 — Rick Incrocci; Kate Salley Palmer

6-7 — Kate Salley Palmer; Kate Salley Palmer; Linda Gist

8-9 — © Jerry Irwin, Photo Researchers*; Janice Skivington; Kate Salley Palmer; Philip Wende

10-11 — © Hermann Schlenker, Zefa Picture Library*; © Photri Alexandra, Robert Harding Picture Library*; Zefa Picture Library*; © Jon Riley, Tony Stone Images*

12-13 — Ian Berry, Magnum*; © J. Bitsch, Zefa Picture Library*; © J. Bitsch, Zefa Picture Library*

14-15 — Philip Wende

16-17 — Janice Skivington; Philip Wende; Janice Skivington; Philip Wende

18-19 — Philip Wende; Philip Wende; Eileen Mueller Neill; Philip Wende; Janice Skivington; Philip Wende

20-21 — © Ed Hoppe*; © John La Due*; © Milton & Joan Mann*; © John La Due†; © M. Serrallier, Photo Researchers*; © Marc & Evelyn Bernheim, Photo Researchers*

22-23 — © Tim Wright, Corbis*; © Photojournalism Japan from Pictorial Parade*

24-25 — © Sabine Weiss, Photo Researchers*; © John Lanois, Black Star*; © Spencer Grant, Photo Researchers*; © Banyan Productions*

26-27 — © Dennis McGilvray; © Ted Spiegal, Black Star*

28-29 — © Robert Harding Picture Library*; © H. K. Bruske, Artstreet*; © Robert Harding Picture Library*; © Horus, Zefa Picture Library*

30-31 — © Robert Harding Picture Library*; © M. Serban, Zefa Picture Library*; © Robert Harding Picture Library*; © Enrico, Zefa Picture Library*; © Lori Adamski-Peek, Tony Stone Images*

32-33 — © Patrisha Thomson, Tony Stone Images*; © David R. Frazier*; Hal French; © David R. Frazier*

34-35 — Janice Skivington

36-37 — Janice Skivington; CHILDCRAFT photo by Donald Getsug; © Bill Ross, Corbis*

38-39 — © Momatiuk/Eastcott from Woodfin Camp Inc.*; © G. Boutin, Zefa Picture Library*; © Dr. P. Thiele, Zefa Picture Agency*

40-41 — © Gerald Cubitt, Bruce Coleman Collection*; © Jerry Irwin, Photo Researchers*; © G. Mabbs, Zefa Picture Library*

42-43 — Kate Salley Palmer

44-45 — © Paul Poplis, Envision*; Peter Geissler; Mike Mogg; Michael Strand

46-47 — © Artstreet*; Peter Geissler; Paul D. Turnbaugh; © Mark Barinholtz*

48-49 — © Sassoon, Robert Harding Picture Library*; © Cathy Melloan*; © G & P Corrigan, Robert Harding Picture Library*; Rick Incrocci

50-51 — © Craig Lovell, Corbis*; Michael Hampshire; © Zefa Picture Library*

52-53 — Mike Mogg; © David Holdsworth, Zefa Picture Library*; Mike Mogg; Mike Mogg; © Cathy Melloan*; © Edward S. Ross*, © G & P Corrigan, Robert Harding Picture Library*

54-55 — © Heinz Steenmans, Zefa Picture Library*; Michael Strand; © Paul Poplis, Envision*; Michael Strand

56-57 — © Jean Pierre Lafont, Liaison*; © Zefa Picture Library*; © Robin Smith, Zefa Picture Library*; © Harrison Forman*

58-59 — © Costa Manos, Magnum*; © Tim Gibson, Envision; © Costa Manos, Magnum*

60-61 — © Robert Davis, Artstreet*; © Jennifer Fry, Bruce Coleman Collection*

62-63 — © Jean L. Briggs, Memorial University, St. Johns, Newfoundland*; © Carl Ostman*; © Anthony Howarth, Woodfin Camp, Inc.*; Richard Orr

64-65 — © David Kay, Robert Harding Picture Library*; Roberta Polfus

66-67 — © Spectrum Colour Library*; © David R. Frazier*; © International Society for Educational Information, Tokyo, Inc.*; © H. Fristedt, Carl Ostman Agency*; Eileen Mueller Neill

68-69 — Jack Lefkowitz

70-77 — Janice Skivington

78-79 — © Liba Taylor, Panos Pictures*; Janice Skivington; Janice Skivington; Steven D. Mach

80-81 — Eileen Mueller Neill; © Spencer Grant, Monkmeyer*; © Jeremy Horner, Corbis*

82-83 — © D. Gratwohl, Zefa Picture Library*

84-85 — Kate Salley Palmer

86-87 — © Kirty McClaren, Zefa Picture Library*; © Cameramann International, Ltd.*; © H. K. Bruske, Artstreet*; © Burt Glinn, Magnum*

88-89 — Kate Salley Palmer

90-91 — © Claudio Villa, Allsport*; © Michael S. Yamashita, Corbis*; © Ian Summer, Robert Harding Picture Library*; © Todd Warshaw, Allsport*; © Bruce Hazelton, Allsport*

92-93 — © Jamie Squire, Allsport*; © Al Bello, Allsport*; © Tony Duffy/NBC from Allsport*; © Mike Hewitt, Allsport*; © Shaun Botterill, Allsport*

94-95 — © Lori Adamski-Peek, Tony Stone Images*; © Paul A. Souders, Corbis*; © David Frazier Photo Library*; Steven D. Mach

96-97 — © David Frazier*; © Jerry Cooke*; © Laurence Fleury, Explorer from Photo Researchers*

98-99 — © Edward S. Ross*; Lynn Cherry; © Cameramann International, Ltd.*

191